VICTIM TO VICTORY

VICTIM TO VICTORY

A SURVIVAL GUIDE TO PERSONAL INJURY

Lawrence LeBrocq, Esq.

BMD PUBLISHING

BMD Publishing
A division of Market Domination LLC

www.MarketDominationLLC.com
BMDPublishing@MarketDominationLLC.com

Copyright © 2025 Lawrence LeBrocq
Victim to Victory: A Survival Guide to Personal Injury

All rights reserved.

Sale of this book without a front cover may be unauthorized. If this book is coverless, it may have been reported to the publisher as "unsold or destroyed" and neither the author nor the publisher has received payment for it.

No part of this publication may be reproduced, stored in a retrieval system, or transmitted in any form or by any means, electronic, mechanical, photocopying, recording, or otherwise, without the prior written permission of the Publisher. Requests to the Publisher for permission should be sent to BMD Publishing, 5888 Main Street, Suite 200, Williamsville, NY 14221.

This book is intended for informational and educational purposes only and should not be considered legal advice. The content of this book is based on the laws and regulations of the United States and may not be applicable in other jurisdictions. Additionally, any information shared in this book is not protected by attorney-client privilege or any other type of confidentiality. Remember, this book is for informational and educational purposes only and should not be considered legal advice.

Printed in the United States of America
ISBN # 9798300687076

BMD PUBLISHING CEO - SETH GREENE
EDITORIAL MANAGEMENT BY CORINA AMBROSE
BOOK DESIGN & LAYOUT BY KRISTIN WILLIAMS

I dedicate this book to my best friend, role model, idol, and best man – my father.

ACKNOWLEDGMENTS

Thank you, Dad, for hiring me as a laborer on a construction site when I was 14 years old. This experience taught me the value of hard work and the value of a dollar. Working 10-hour days every summer and during school breaks for nine years as a laborer, framer, and crew chief hardened my resolve to work hard and excel. My father taught me how to live, love, work, and die.

My Pop was a big man with a bigger heart. At 6'3" and 280 pounds, he was a gentle giant. He never met a person he disliked and could always see the good in everyone. He was a baseball coach for over twenty years and was always available to anyone who needed help at any time.

My Dad was a member of the Asbestos Union in the '60s and blew asbestos insulation in the nuclear power plants in New York. I remember him leaving for work every day before dawn and never getting home until after 7 p.m. He described the job as working in a snow globe, with asbestos flying everywhere.

The survival rate of Mesothelioma victims is zero. The hardest part for someone suffering from Mesothelioma is the lack of hope for survival.

My father died at the age of 63 from Mesothelioma, which is a type of cancer only caused by asbestos. The tragic part of this is the industry leaders knew asbestos was deadly, but because it was inexpensive and the profit margins were so high, they continued to use the product. In essence, the asbestos industry sacrificed human life for financial profits.

On his deathbed, my father was troubled because he did not leave my family any money, but I assured him the amount of love and comfort he provided was more valuable than any amount of money. I assured him my sister and I were more than capable of providing for ourselves and our mother. The irony is in death, my father's lawsuit against the Asbestos companies allowed my mother to receive a substantial settlement. However, no sum of money can bring a person back from the grave or is sufficient to restore a person to where they were before the injury.

My path from blue-collar construction worker to lawyer requires additional people to thank and recognize. I must thank my mother, who told me since I was young that I would make a good lawyer even though no one in my family had ever gone to college. I want to thank my coach, Jim Muldowney, who helped me get an athletic scholarship to college. Without his help, I could not have afforded to attend college. My college guidance counselor suggested that with my grades, along with a history major with a minor in political science, I could get into law school. This was the first time I seriously considered the option, even though I had already been offered a position as a teacher and coach at a local high school. My three children, Cody, Tyler, and Brianna who inspire and motivate me to be the best father, mentor, and lawyer I can be.

I am grateful for the opportunity, confidence, and trust my two partners, Will Garces and Bill Grabler, have shown in me by making me the managing partner of GGL. Their support has enabled our team to

ACKNOWLEDGMENTS

significantly improve our culture, processes, and procedures. By applying industry best practices, we have become a leader in the legal profession, resolving over 100 million dollars in verdicts and settlements annually, and have been named one of the Best Law Firms to work for by US News and World Reports. Finally, thank you to Seth Greene, Corina Ambrose, Kristin Williams, and Dawn-Michelle Lewis for making this book possible. I couldn't have completed it without the fantastic team at Market Domination.

CONTENTS

Acknowledgments vii

Introduction 1

Meet Lawrence 3

Chapter 1 | Essential Steps to Take Following a PI Incident . 11

Chapter 2 | How to Find a Winning Attorney 17

Chapter 3 | Why Choose a Chiropractor 35

Chapter 4 | The Role of the Pain Management Doctor 47

Chapter 5 | The Role of an Orthopedist 59

Chapter 6 | When to See a Neurologist 71

Chapter 7 | How Economists Prove Financial Losses 85

Chapter 8 | How to Avoid Being a Victim in Your PI Case ... 93

What's Next? 101

INTRODUCTION

YOU MIGHT BE WONDERING, "Why should I read a book about personal injury?" Maybe you've never been injured at work or had a personal injury, or maybe you have but you simply took the pay out from your boss or an insurance company.

The fact of the matter is, anyone can be involved in a personal injury at any time. You might be driving home from dinner, and you get hit by a drunk driver. You might experience a slip and fall at work. Personal injury doesn't discriminate.

Even with everything I have learned during my years of being a personal injury attorney, I am always looking for new ways to help my clients get back to living a normal life. That's why I interviewed personal injury attorneys, chiropractors, pain management doctors, orthopedists, neurosurgeons, and an economic expert.

Having an injury isn't something you plan for and can be one of the most challenging things you can go through. I help my clients navigate through this process to ensure they get the outcome they deserve. If you've been injured, it is vital that you hire a personal injury attorney to do the same for you.

Figuring out what to do during the aftermath of an injury can feel overwhelming and uncertain, especially when you're unsure of the steps to take to protect your rights and well-being. This is where having the right guidance becomes crucial. Just as I support my clients through every phase of their personal injury cases, I wanted to create a resource that offers the same level of support to anyone facing similar challenges.

I wrote this book to help guide those who have experienced a work-related injury or a personal injury. My goal was to address questions you might have regarding what steps you should take after being injured. I wanted to share my expertise and give you the assurance you need to take important steps in your personal injury case, whether that's seeing a chiropractor or a neurosurgeon. Regardless of the injury you've experienced, this book will help you make informed decisions while going through one of the most difficult times in your life.

MEET LAWRENCE

BEFORE YOU HEAR from the professionals I interviewed for this book, I'd like you to learn a little about me. Understanding how I got to this point in my career and life will help you get more out of these interviews.

I come from humble beginnings, so a strong work ethic was instilled in me at an early age. My parents were young and had very little money. When I turned seven, they were able to purchase a tiny house for our family, but they couldn't afford furniture for another two years, so we sat on lawn chairs. Once I turned 14, I started working full-time in the summers and during other school breaks.

Even though my grades in high school weren't excellent, I was lucky enough to get an athletic scholarship to attend college. After arriving, I met a woman who was jealous of my scholarship because she didn't have one and received better grades than me in high school. She said, "Your scholarship doesn't matter because you're going to flunk out anyway." That really stuck with me. At that moment, I realized she might be right. This interaction inspired me to study as hard as possible and get good grades. Due to my diligent studying, I ended up on the Dean's List and stayed there for the rest of college. I eventually received an academic scholarship.

During college, I never pictured myself as a lawyer. I was majoring in secondary education and history, and I planned to become a teacher and a coach. My guidance counselor suggested going to law school as a good option because I minored in Political Science, had good grades, and had a good shot at getting a scholarship. I told him that if someone paid for me to go to law school, I would attend. That's how I ended up going to law school at Mississippi College.

After law school, I went on to receive an LLM in International Business Finance from the University of London, King's College, London School of Economics. I practiced international law for a couple of years. My journey included stops in Salzburg, London, and Bangkok. My last position was with Coudert Brothers in Bangkok, but I could only work for them overseas because I didn't attend a top-tier law school in the United States. It didn't matter that I went to the top-ranked law school in the world for international business law. So, when they offered me a permanent position in Vietnam, I decided I didn't want to spend my life there and returned to the United States.

When I returned to the U.S., I decided to open my own firm. In the beginning, I worked as a lawyer by day and had a full-time job at night. I took any case that came my way because I was not only trying to build my practice but also needed the income. Then, a friend of mine got in a significant automobile collision and was seriously injured. I ended up getting him $408,000 on my first-ever personal injury case. I took the money I earned in that case, put a down payment on a building, which we still use today as one of our twelve offices, and began doing more personal injury cases.

I went from being a solo practitioner to forming a partnership called Burns, LeBrocq, and Wolf. I specialized in personal injury, while one partner focused on elder law and the other specialized in corporate and matrimonial law. After receiving three outstanding verdicts during the summer of 2006, Will Garces made me an offer I couldn't refuse. Even my partners agreed I had to take it. So, in January 2007, I moved to Garces and Grabler. Eventually, that became Garces, Grabler, and LeBrocq (GGL), and I took over the personal injury department.

The most important thing to me as a litigator was maximizing the value of every claim. We do this by preparing for trial. Personal injury cases can become quite expensive, as getting reports and testimony from doctors and experts alone can cost $25,000. I once had a case that cost me $70,000 to prepare and then $70,000 more to bring the experts in during the trial. Spending that money wasn't an issue because it allowed me to maximize the case's value and give my client the best chance to succeed. The case resolved for a substantial amount of money which I cannot disclose because of a Non-Disclosure Agreement with the defendant.

That's what differentiates us from everybody else. I have over 36 years of experience. I've been an arbitrator for the court going on 30 years. The courts trust me to set the value of a case. I set the value on every case in our firm, and no one can settle the case for less without my approval. I never want to undervalue a case. If anybody under-settles a case, they will be terminated on the spot. Refusing never to undervalue cases and never to hurt clients separates us from our competitors. In fact, because of our stellar reputation, top litigators want to be part of our team so we no longer have to recruit. Good like-minded people want to come and work for us.

I enjoy working in personal injury because I can really make a difference in people's lives. For example, there is one case that I will never forget. A 19-year-old woman was the passenger in her boyfriend's vehicle. He was driving her home after date night when they were T-boned by a 17-year-old who was very intoxicated. He ran through two stop signs before hitting their vehicle. The young woman had fallen asleep on the drive home and was resting her head on the door where they were struck.

They were hit so hard that the car rolled over, and she was hanging upside down through the broken glass while her seatbelt held her in place. The impact was so severe she had a hole where her nose and mouth used to be. Her teeth and nose were gone, and in addition to that, she had significant orthopedic injuries. Amazingly, she survived.

The seventeen-year-old who hit her only had a $15,000 policy, and she had what's called underinsured motorist coverage through her parents' insurance for $250,000. I knew that the total amount of $265,000 wasn't nearly enough. Through investigation and depositions, my team and I were able to learn that the other driver had been drinking at two different houses before the crash. We had to prove he was drinking or had open access to alcohol at their homes. Because we were able to prove the defendant consumed alcohol at the two different homes, we could use the homeowner's insurance from each place he consumed alcohol. As a result, this young woman received a significant settlement. Her boyfriend's total policy was also turned over even though he only had a small level of liability for the car crash.

This case affected me emotionally because I was so in awe of this young woman. Her pelvis was broken, and she had many other fractures. Her face was gone. Even after reconstructive surgery, she couldn't rest her chin on her hand because her jaw would collapse. She never stopped going to school despite all the orthopedic and reconstructive surgeries she needed. She graduated from college, eventually had a child, and lives fully. I'll never forget her strength of character, and I was happy to get her the settlement she deserved.

In another case, I represented a man who had burned 80% of his body while he was working. He had been assigned to scrape the polyurethane off hardwood floors using acetone. Acetone is highly flammable, and there was even a meeting to remind management of the importance of turning off all pilot lights. However, his supervisor forgot to turn off the pilot light to a hot water heater. Because the pilot light was not turned off, the contact with the acetone fumes caused an explosion that sent this man out the window of a third-story apartment, leaving him almost completely burned with many orthopedic injuries.

When he was taken to the hospital, the doctors didn't think he would survive the burns, so they didn't treat his other injuries. Well, the man survived, and the doctors had to fix his orthopedic injuries as well. We worked on this case for eight years to get our client the compensation he deserved. His employer said it was simply a worker's compensation claim and denied the negligence claim. So, we went into mediation on the negligence claim. The defense flew in top lawyers from around the country – Chicago, Los Angeles, and Houston – who came in saying they wouldn't pay a dime. One of my associates who had been working on the case the whole time broke down and wanted to end the mediation. So, I took over.

I immersed myself with the case, going through excruciatingly painful details about what this man suffered, including explaining how his genitalia were burned off. At the time of the mediation the defense had made a motion to dismiss the case pursuant to the Workers Compensation bar. With the motion pending, I told the defense if they wanted to go to court on the chance that a judge would throw the case out, they could take that risk. I explained, however, we had enough evidence to get past the motion to dismiss the case on the Workers Compensation Bar based upon what's called a "Laidlow claim,". A "Laidlow claim" holds that if the employers' action or inaction is so reckless or intentional and there is a significant danger of a severe injury, you can still file a claim against your employer in Superior Court as well as in worker's compensation court. I told them our demand was $25 million and would never be a penny less than that. They immediately came up with a seven-figure offer that the client wanted to take. We talked the client out of taking that money and told him we would get him more. We ended up settling for several million dollars in Superior Court and settled with worker's compensation insurance carrier to include having his medical bills paid for life. We succeeded in both our worker compensation and Superior Court claims.

These two cases show that I really strive to get the best outcomes for my clients. That's one reason so many of our cases result from referrals from previous clients. If you treat people very well, they will come back to you in the future.

While writing this book, I learned that the top people in the legal industry think the way I do. They're driven, disciplined in all aspects of life, and really care about and have deep concern and empathy for their clients. Because of this, they strive to do what is best for their clients by listening and doing all the work necessary to get them the best outcome possible.

I decided to write this book for anyone who has been injured, whether or not they file a lawsuit. I want people who have been injured by somebody else's negligence to know that there is help for them and that they aren't alone. I wanted to create a guide that helps people, whether they have been hurt or are helping someone who has been hurt, navigate the legal system, specifically personal injury.

This is also an excellent resource for anyone considering becoming a personal injury lawyer. It gives an idea of what the best in the business are doing and provides examples of cases a lawyer might encounter.

Doctors treating injured people can learn a lot from this book as well. PIP laws dictate how a doctor gets paid. Treating someone involved in an automobile collision is very different from treating a patient who wasn't in a car crash because the doctor gets paid differently. They can't just use the patient's health insurance; they must go through the auto insurance fee schedule. If someone doesn't have auto or health insurance, he needs a letter of protection from a lawyer saying they will protect his bill in the settlement. The doctor will not be paid the same as he would have been paid through health insurance. They will be paid the usual and customary rate in the industry. Doctors need to be educated on this if they are going to treat injured victims.

Overall, I want victims to know there are lawyers on their side who want to help fight their legal battles. Getting in a car crash, slip and fall, or getting injured at work shouldn't limit what people can achieve in the future. People have the right to know what help is available to them and should be represented whether they were injured at work, in a car collision, had a slip and fall, or were hurt at a construction site. The fact of the matter is, when dealing with these kinds of cases, people need lawyers to help steer them to the best possible outcome.

Now, let's begin.

Chapter 1

ESSENTIAL STEPS TO TAKE FOLLOWING A PERSONAL INJURY INCIDENT

BEING INVOLVED IN A PERSONAL INJURY INCIDENT is a life-altering experience. Whether it's a car collision, a slip and fall, or any other type of injury, the impact can be devastating—physically, emotionally, and financially. The steps you take immediately after the incident can significantly affect the outcome of your case and your recovery. This chapter will guide you through what to do if you find yourself in such a situation, helping you navigate the complex legal landscape and maximize your chances of receiving fair compensation.

Your health is your most important priority. Even if you feel fine after being injured, seeking medical attention right away is crucial. Some injuries, such as internal bleeding or concussions, may not be immediately apparent but can have severe consequences if left untreated. Additionally, having a medical record of your injuries is essential for your personal injury case. It provides evidence that links your injuries directly to the incident, which is crucial when seeking compensation.

Once you've addressed your immediate health concerns, it's essential to turn your attention to securing your legal rights. Building a solid personal injury case begins with thorough documentation, which plays a critical role in substantiating your claims and ensuring you receive the compensation you deserve. Documentation is essential to a personal injury case. As soon as you can, start gathering evidence related to the incident. This includes taking photographs of the scene, your injuries, and any property damage. If there were witnesses, try to get their contact information, as their statements could support your case.

Whether it's a car collision, a workplace injury, or any other type of incident, report the incident to the appropriate authorities. For car crashes, this means calling the police. For workplace injuries, notify your employer immediately and make sure you fill out an incident report. An official report is another essential piece of documentation that can support your case. Ensure that the report is accurate and includes all relevant details.

Once you've reported the incident to the appropriate authorities, you must be cautious about who you speak with and what you say. While it's natural to want to discuss the incident, especially with insurance adjusters, it's crucial to remember that these conversations can significantly impact the outcome of your claim.

One of the most common mistakes personal injury victims make is speaking too freely with insurance adjusters. Remember, the adjuster's job is to minimize the value of your claim. Anything you say can and will be used against you later. For instance, if you downplay your injuries by saying, "I just have some aches and pains," the insurance company may use that statement to justify a lower settlement offer.

In the words of an experienced lawyer, the insurance adjuster is not your friend; they are your adversary. If asked whether you were injured, state, "Yes, I was injured." For any further inquiries, direct them to your attorney. This approach protects your interests and prevents the adjuster from twisting your words to minimize your claim.

By maintaining caution in your communications with insurance adjusters, you're taking a crucial step in safeguarding your claim. However, successfully understanding the complexities of the legal system requires more than just careful communication; it demands expert guidance. This is where the value of hiring a qualified personal injury lawyer becomes evident.

Navigating the legal system alone is incredibly challenging, especially when dealing with insurance companies that are determined to pay out as little as possible. Hiring a personal injury lawyer is one of the most important steps you can take. For example, a certified civil trial lawyer specializes in personal injury cases and has the expertise to build a strong case on your behalf.

As discussed earlier, it's essential to work with a specialist. Just as you wouldn't go to a general practitioner for brain surgery, you shouldn't rely on a lawyer who dabbles in various fields for a severe personal injury case. A certified trial lawyer has the experience and knowledge to fight for the compensation you deserve.

Insurance companies are in the business of making money, and their primary goal is to protect their bottom line. They will often employ tactics to delay or minimize your payout. For example, they might offer you a lowball settlement early on, hoping you'll accept it out of desperation. Being patient and resisting the urge to settle too quickly is essential.

I have worked on a case where the insurance company's final offer was $50,000, but through persistence and skilled lawyering, the final verdict was $3.1 million. The insurance company's strategy was to wear down the victim with low offers, but the case's actual value was realized and achieved with proper legal representation.

Personal injury cases can take time, especially if they go to trial. Being mentally and emotionally prepared for a potentially lengthy process is important. Insurance companies often drag their feet, hoping you'll settle for less to get the ordeal over with, making your patience pay off in the long run.

I have dealt with cases that took several years to settle. Despite the lengthy process, thorough preparation and strategic lawyering will ultimately lead to a better outcome. That outcome is only possible when your legal team is prepared to take the case to trial if necessary.

Every personal injury case is unique, and the legal options available will depend on your situation's specifics. For example, you can't sue your employer for negligence in New Jersey unless it's an egregious act. However, other avenues often exist to explore, such as filing claims against third parties or pursuing workers' compensation benefits.

Understanding your rights and the legal landscape is crucial. A qualified personal injury lawyer can explain your options and help you make informed decisions. While your legal team handles the complexities of your case, it's important to focus on your recovery. Follow your doctor's advice, attend all medical appointments, and prioritize your health. Document your recovery process, including any physical or emotional challenges you face. This information can be valuable in supporting your compensation claim.

The journey to recovery after a personal injury is often difficult, both physically and emotionally. I've seen firsthand how clients who prioritize their healing while entrusting their legal matters to experienced professionals can achieve remarkable results. As you focus on your recovery, you must be prepared for the next phase of your case—the settlement.

Most personal injury cases are settled out of court, but preparing for the settlement process is important. Your lawyer will negotiate with the insurance company on your behalf, but ultimately, the decision to accept or reject a settlement offer is yours. It's essential to carefully consider any offer and consult with your lawyer before making a decision.

ESSENTIAL STEPS TO TAKE

Remember, the goal is to secure fair compensation that covers your medical expenses, lost wages, pain and suffering, and any other damages you've incurred. If the insurance company's offer doesn't reflect the actual value of your case, be prepared to take the case to trial.

Being a personal injury victim is a daunting experience. Still, with the proper steps and legal representation, you can navigate this challenging time and secure the compensation you deserve. From seeking immediate medical attention to hiring a qualified personal injury lawyer, each step is crucial in building a solid case and maximizing your chances of a successful outcome.

Remember, you don't have to go through this alone. A skilled personal injury lawyer can guide you through the process, protect your rights, and fight for the compensation you need to move forward with your life. Whether your case is resolved through settlement or goes to trial, the goal is to help you achieve the best possible outcome.

TAKEAWAYS FROM THIS CHAPTER

1. Immediate Medical Attention is Crucial: After any personal injury incident, seeking prompt medical care is essential, even if you feel fine. Some injuries may not be immediately apparent, and having a medical record is vital for linking your injuries to the crash in your personal injury case.

2. Document Everything: Thorough documentation is critical to building a solid personal injury case. This includes photographing the collision scene, your injuries, and any property damage, collecting witness information, and filing official reports with the appropriate authorities.

3. Be Cautious with Insurance Adjusters: Insurance adjusters are not your allies. They aim to minimize the value of your claim, so be careful with your words. Direct all inquiries to your lawyer to protect your interests and avoid having your statements used against you.

4. Hire a Qualified Personal Injury Lawyer: Navigating the legal system and dealing with insurance companies can be overwhelming. A specialized personal injury lawyer can guide you through the process, build a strong case, and fight for the compensation you deserve.

5. Patience Pays Off: Personal injury cases can be lengthy, especially if they go to trial. Being patient and prepared for a potentially lengthy process is essential, as persistence and thorough legal representation can lead to a better outcome.

Chapter 2

HOW TO FIND A WINNING ATTORNEY

"An injured person should take steps to protect their rights. The first thing they should do is get a lawyer, and getting the right lawyer is crucial."

— MICHAEL ADLER

AFTER OBTAINING A PERSONAL INJURY, hiring a lawyer is one of the most important things you can do. That's why I spoke to different personal injury lawyers about helping people find the best attorney for their situation and why having the help of an expert is in your best interest. Unfortunately, many people don't contact an attorney after a car collision or a work incident. This is a mistake because insurance companies will try to pay out as little as possible. Hiring someone to represent you is the best decision you can make. After a personal injury, you must hire a lawyer to receive the compensation you deserve.

Many people don't feel comfortable contacting an attorney for various reasons. Often, they fear they cannot afford one. However, this fear should not prevent individuals from obtaining a lawyer after a personal injury. Joshua Brumley explains that personal injury lawyers work on a contingency fee basis, so there is no reason to avoid seeking legal counsel: "People are terrified to engage an attorney, first and foremost, because they worry about the cost. When they find out that all personal injury attorneys work on a contingency fee basis, where they only get paid a percentage at the end of the case, that fear disappears."

Jon Groth also discussed the fear component, and he agrees that the fear of having to pay up-front is not something people should be worried about after a personal injury: "People need to realize that our interests are aligned with theirs—we aim to secure as much compensation as possible, and we don't get paid until the end of the case. There's no upfront payment; you may sign an agreement or a retainer document, but it doesn't mean you're writing a check to the attorney immediately, as that wouldn't be practical. Imagine an injured victim who is unable to work for weeks or months; they would never be able to afford an attorney if they had to pay upfront." Groth notes, "This misconception acts as a barrier to justice because people may receive misinformation from insurance companies or elsewhere, leading to hesitation in contacting lawyers."

Unfortunately, as Thomas Giordano, Jr. points out, "People are so reluctant to contact a lawyer that they allow manipulation to occur by the insurance company and the adjusters." By hiring a lawyer, Giordano argues, "It allows you to go up against the insurance company with their endless pockets, feeling like you're on an equal playing field." Brumley agrees that people shouldn't try to take on insurance companies alone: "If you negotiate on your own without experience negotiating against insurance companies, you're probably leaving money on the table." He explains, "If you don't want to get scammed by an insurance company, you must have a lawyer. Insurance companies are businesses, and businesses exist to make profits. While the person on the phone might sound sweet and ask if you're okay, their job is to protect the insurance company's money, not to pay you more. An attorney's job is to get that insurance company to pull out the bigger checkbook and compensate you fairly." That is why hiring the right attorney to represent you is paramount.

Bill Biggs agrees that many people make the mistake of trusting insurance companies. He notes, "The insurance company is not on your side. Their business model relies on collecting premiums and minimizing payouts." Clients should avoid relying on insurance companies and seek an experienced lawyer for the best chance at a fair outcome.

Insurance companies have standard responses for some instances and collisions. In car crash cases, Brumley points out, "An insurance adjuster will offer amounts like $500, $1,000, or $1,500. However, after clients retain us, we often resolve their cases for $25,000 to $50,000. This pattern is a regular occurrence, and while each case is unique, there are similarities in how insurance companies treat these cases and the standard responses they give during negotiations. We have developed responses to overcome these objections, obtain policy limit information, and ensure our clients receive the compensation they deserve."

So, while you may consider this biased advice coming from a personal injury attorney, I believe it's evident that hiring a lawyer after being a victim of personal injury is one of the most intelligent choices you can make. Brumley tells us the numbers speak for themselves: "There is mathematical data that shows people get over 10 times more money using an attorney than they do by themselves."

Finding the right personal injury attorney can make a massive difference in both the outcome of your case and the experience of going through it. As Biggs explains, "It has a huge impact. I would break down performance into two categories for the client, focusing on what they're looking for and how it affects them." These two categories—technical expertise and client communication—are foundational when selecting an attorney.

It might be difficult, however, to know what lawyer to choose or where to start when finding representation. You want to avoid going to a jack of all trades. After all, you shouldn't hire a criminal lawyer for a personal injury case. You want to hire someone knowledgeable about whatever incident you've been in. Whether it's a car collision, a slip and fall, or an incident at work, the lawyer who works on your case should be an expert in that area.

This is also important from the attorney's perspective. As Groth points out, specializing in a particular area of law will lead to a better outcome for your client: "Unlike attorneys who may handle a variety of cases, including wills, business formations, and personal injury, our focus allows us to delve deeply not only into the facts of each case but also into the strategic aspects of maximizing recovery for the victim. This focused approach gives us a distinct advantage in achieving the best outcomes for our clients."

It's crucial to consider an attorney's skill level and experience. Biggs notes, "Our team desires good performance and service—specifically in their legal decision-making, the lawyer's expertise, and how well they execute their craft." A strong attorney should be able to make sound legal decisions, handle the complexities of the law, and possess the assertiveness to advocate fiercely for you. In personal injury cases, this aggressive advocacy can make all the difference in recovering maximum compensation. A culture of passion and assertiveness, as Biggs points out, often leads to "better, more substantial recoveries for the client."

Another critical aspect is what Biggs calls the "bedside manner" of the attorney. Communication is essential, and poor communication is the top complaint from clients. According to Biggs, "The number one issue clients raise in surveys—their top complaint about working with a personal injury or workers' comp law firm—is communication or the lack of it." Clients want to feel heard, informed, and assured that their attorney is working for their best interest. An attorney should be responsive, keeping you updated with regular case progress reports and setting clear expectations about the process and potential outcomes.

When someone is dealing with a personal injury case, it's likely a new experience. Tim McKey emphasizes the importance of attorneys who can clearly explain the case process in simple terms. "Lawyers should clearly outline the steps involved. They need to feel empathy and have someone explain the process in layman's terms," he says. A reasonable attorney understands that, for most clients, this is unfamiliar territory. You need an attorney who takes the time to break down legal jargon, provide guidance, and genuinely empathize with your situation.

McKey believes that relationships are at the heart of quality legal representation. "Relationships are the most important aspect, not just in business but in life. Paying close attention to them is essential," he states. When evaluating a law firm, look for one that prioritizes client relationships. You want an attorney who sees you as more than a case number, someone who understands that trust is earned by consistently being there for you throughout the legal process.

The two most important factors in maximizing the value of a case are the attorney you choose and their communication with you. Clear communication allows attorneys to empathize with their clients.

McKey points out that regular contact with clients can significantly impact the value of a case. "Consistent, periodic contact with clients is a crucial driver of case value," he explains. Reasonable attorneys check in with their clients regularly, ensuring they follow up on medical treatment, address new needs, and provide reassurance. This keeps clients informed and helps strengthen the case by ensuring no critical details are overlooked.

Choosing the right lawyer is not something to be taken lightly. Research should be done before you choose your attorney. Ken Hardison argues that researching lawyers to select the right one for you is crucial: "When people choose a lawyer, it's akin to selecting a brain surgeon—a crucial decision that can significantly impact their lives. While for us, it's a routine part of our work, for them, it's a major event. Just as one would meticulously research and vet a brain surgeon, individuals should conduct due diligence when selecting an attorney. This includes asking questions, having discussions, reviewing testimonials, and checking with the relevant professional boards for any violations or censures related to client matters."

It's easy to get drawn in by flashy ads, but McKey warns that effective marketing is only one piece of the puzzle. "The 'steak' has to be good—it can't just be all sizzle," he explains. When selecting a law firm, ensure they have experienced attorneys with the necessary education and skills to handle your case effectively. Look beyond the marketing to see if they have a reputation for delivering quality legal work.

Advertising can introduce a law firm, but trust is built through genuine connection. McKey explains, "Clients are looking for someone they can trust and who shows empathy and understanding." When choosing a personal injury attorney, look beyond the advertisements to find a firm that feels approachable and compassionate. This personal connection is crucial in fostering trust and ensuring you feel supported throughout your case.

Michael Mogill highlights that many clients struggle to differentiate between law firms because they all make similar claims, such as being "the best" or having awards like "Super Lawyer." From a client's perspective, Mogill notes, "It's largely an emotional choice." Clients often rely on personal factors like Google reviews, word of mouth, or a firm's community involvement. As Mogill explains, "Simply claiming to be 'the best' isn't enough, as every firm makes that claim." Therefore, choosing an attorney who can establish a genuine connection is essential. Lawyers who communicate a unique purpose, share their stories, and are involved in their community often build a stronger bond with potential clients.

What else goes into the decision? Hardison argues, "You want to consider someone with a proven winning track record. You can gauge this by looking at their reviews, but it's important to not just glance at them but read them thoroughly. Additionally, you should talk to the attorney to see if they are a good fit."

Many personal injury lawyers recommend that clients research attorneys and do their due diligence before selecting one. It could be as easy as checking Google reviews to see if a lawyer might be a good fit. Giordano points out, "We live in this world where I can Google personal injury attorneys, find out about them, and see what they've done. You can find out their accomplishments with a one-minute search."

Researching to find the best lawyer for your case is one of the most important things you can do. As Adler points out, "Investing time upfront to find a higher-quality lawyer is probably the most important factor in adequately compensating for something that's been taken from you." You must be diligent while doing your research. Some firms make patently false claims. For example, Adler notes, "There is no official ranking system for lawyers and law firms. When they boast about 'recovering $500 million,' it's important to read the fine print because it's typically the entire firm's recoveries, not just one lawyer's. Instead, check Google reviews. Don't just look at the first ten entries; dig into the next 20 for a more balanced view."

It's also important to remember that you want to work with a personal injury attorney that you like and trust. The trust factor comes when you find the right fit. You want to go to a lawyer who treats you like family and puts you first. When selecting an attorney, consider whether they are authentic and relatable. Mogill believes establishing a "know, like, and trust" relationship is key: "If they don't know you, they can't hire you… if they don't like you, they won't hire you…if they don't trust you, they won't sign on." A lawyer's personality, approachability, and connection with clients are just as vital as their legal qualifications.

This isn't a relationship that's ending in six months. It could take several years before everything is settled. Groth explains, "I tell potential clients that we could have a short-term or a long-term relationship. They need to understand my perspective and get a sense of who I am, as we could be in communication for the next few years. I want them to feel comfortable sharing everything with me as their lawyer, attorney, and counselor at law. Our discussions might involve very personal matters, which is necessary for me to advocate effectively on their behalf. They need to know that the law firm can be there for them in the long term and that they have a good feeling about the lawyer they'll be working with for an extended period." To have those difficult conversations, you need to have a lawyer you feel comfortable confiding in. Groth notes, one way to establish that trust, "is through face-to-face interactions, which allow me to educate clients about the process and help them understand my perspective and how I can assist them."

Plaintiff law firms and lawyers must speak with their clients frequently. This practice should develop empathy and help them understand their client more. It also keeps the client in line with how the lawsuit progresses so they don't feel in the dark and are more willing to open up. McKey agrees: "Clients are looking for someone they can trust to handle a serious matter, which they probably didn't want to be in, to begin with. They want someone with empathy for their situation."

The personal injury lawyer you hire should fight for your best interests. As Hardison argues, "Everything you do should be for the benefit of the client." Michael Adler agrees: "We fight to the death for our clients, and we make a meaningful difference in many people's lives." Just because someone has a billboard ad doesn't mean they are the best lawyer to represent you. In fact, the opposite might be true. As Adler argues, "In many cases, the big advertising firms who advertise on billboards have a system that actually goes against many people's best interests. They have to pay for that advertising bill, and as more cases come in, they have a finite number of resources to work with. So, when 200 more cases come in, they have to close 200 cases. This often means they don't go the extra mile or fight for additional compensation; they want to churn and burn." Adler suggests, "Asking around and getting referrals is way more important than calling a number or name you see on a billboard."

Mogill argues that there are three main elements a successful law firm should possess: differentiation, visibility, and a solid business foundation. He explains, "There are three main components. We help law firms differentiate and stand out by uncovering their story, unique value proposition, and message." Beyond that, it's essential to "get known" by placing content strategically on the platforms clients frequent, like LinkedIn, Facebook, or YouTube, depending on the target audience. As Mogill puts it, "You can't get hired if you're the best-kept secret." Seek a firm that stands out for the right reasons, blending skill with a personal touch.

Law firms must differentiate themselves not only through expertise but also through personality. Mogill says, "Differentiation isn't necessarily about being better; it's about being distinct." Look for a lawyer who stands out for their story, values, and unique reasons for practicing law. Sharing elements like why they chose this field, their involvement in the community, or their passion for justice can make a law firm more relatable. Understanding the value of a visible community presence and direct client connections is crucial. It helps potential clients see them as more than just lawyers.

Lastly, the law firm's internal structure matters as much as its external appearance. Mogill advises starting with a strong foundation: attracting great talent, developing efficient processes, and using data and reporting to improve client experience. As he points out, marketing alone won't solve problems within the firm. "If your practice lacks structure, pouring on more marketing will only add to existing issues."

Efficiency isn't just about saving time; it's about providing high-quality service in a streamlined way. McKey stresses the importance of efficient systems, stating, "Our job is to help you deliver those services more efficiently and effectively." An efficient firm respects your time and handles each step of the legal process with precision and organization, helping you feel confident that your case is in capable hands.

You won't regret hiring a lawyer familiar with your hometown and the insurance laws in your state. As Groth explains, "Certain aspects are unique to the state, particularly within the realm of personal injury. The analysis required, such as determining if a phantom vehicle was involved or underinsured motorist coverage applies, as well as the best approach to maximizing recovery through health insurance versus other means, is something we deal with daily." This practice allows us to refine our skills and develop a deep understanding of optimizing recovery for our clients.

Before finalizing your choice, have an open and candid conversation with potential attorneys. If you experience issues such as poor communication, don't hesitate to address them directly. "Sometimes, issues stem from miscommunication; other times, it's a lack of communication altogether," Biggs observes. Setting the right expectations upfront allows clients to avoid frustration and confusion later in the process.

Groth argues that just as regular communication from lawyer to client is essential, it's a two-way street: "Keeping us informed about your situation helps us support you better. If you need to change doctors or if your current doctor recommends a different facility, please inform us of your plans. There are instances where certain doctors are reluctant to work with lawyers, even if they are highly recommended specialists. If you receive referrals, consulting with us beforehand can ensure that you choose a doctor who will provide excellent care and support your legal case if needed."

An excellent personal injury attorney will know which doctors will testify on your behalf and which won't. This is vital information to have when going to trial. As Groth notes, "That's where we can provide additional value because lawyers who specialize in this area develop a sense of which doctors prefer not to be involved in legal matters." This is crucial as Biggs explains, "You deserve to have any future health issues considered as part of your recovery." Injury recovery can often extend beyond the initial treatment period, and an effective attorney will ensure future medical needs are accounted for in any settlement.

Being open and honest with your lawyer is crucial for your lawyer to get the compensation you deserve. Listening to your personal injury lawyer's advice is also vital. Groth says it's helpful for people to know they aren't alone in this process: "You're not alone when it comes to the stress caused by the insurance process. We can be there for you. Many lawyers in offices across the nation have handled situations like yours. We can answer questions to hopefully alleviate some of that stress."

Don't try to navigate insurance policies by yourself after getting injured. Instead, do your due diligence and find the right personal injury attorney for your case. The insurance companies are not your friends, and finding representation after a personal injury is the smartest thing you can do. I hope these tips help you find the best lawyer for your case.

Choosing the right personal injury attorney requires more than reviewing awards or ads. Look for an attorney who combines technical skills with compassion, communicates effectively, and builds trust through genuine connection. By researching, setting clear expectations, and avoiding common pitfalls, you can find a lawyer to achieve the best possible outcome for your case and make the journey as smooth as possible.

TAKEAWAYS FROM THIS CHAPTER

1. Hire a Lawyer Quickly to Protect Your Rights: Securing a lawyer is critical to ensuring you receive fair compensation after a personal injury. Insurance companies aim to minimize payouts, so having a lawyer on your side levels the playing field.

2. Understand Contingency Fees: Many people hesitate to hire a personal injury lawyer due to cost concerns. However, most personal injury attorneys work on a contingency fee basis, meaning they only get paid if you win. This eliminates upfront costs and aligns the lawyer's interests with yours.

3. Choose a Specialist in Personal Injury Law: Look for an attorney specializing in personal injury cases, as they will have the focused knowledge and skills to maximize recovery. Avoid generalists who handle various case types; a specialized attorney will better understand the nuances and strategies required for personal injury cases.

4. Look Beyond Advertising: Advertising alone isn't enough to judge a lawyer's quality. Big advertising firms may handle high volumes of cases, which can lead to rushed settlements. Instead, ask for referrals, read reviews, and choose a lawyer known for both skill and genuine client care.

5. Prioritize Communication and Empathy: Good attorneys keep clients informed, provide regular updates, and foster a sense of trust. Clear communication, empathy, and a strong client relationship are crucial for a positive legal experience, especially in personal injury cases where clients may feel vulnerable.

Joshua Brumley is a Washington State native who was raised in the Tacoma area. After graduating from the University of Washington, he earned his MBA at Jacksonville University and completed his law degree at Florida Coastal School of Law. Joshua has practiced as an attorney with the Washington State Bar Association since 2015. He has served as a pro-tem judge and owns Brumley Law Firm, whose mission is to "empower our community by providing client-focused service, one car crash at a time."

As the managing attorney at Brumley Law Firm, Joshua works daily to ensure the team delivers the most professional and supportive legal services in Western Washington. His peers have recognized him in the select group of Rising Stars of the 2020, 2021, 2022, and 2023 Super Lawyers survey.

— WWW.BRUMLEYLAWFIRM.COM —

Jon Groth, a seasoned attorney, graduated from Marquette Law School in 2000 and has since dedicated his career to Wisconsin litigation and personal injury law. As the founder of Groth Law Firm, Jon has successfully handled a wide range of cases, including auto collisions, product liability, nursing home neglect, and civil litigation.

Jon understands the importance of empathy and dedication in serving his clients. His legal expertise has earned him numerous accolades, including being named a Rising Star, a SuperLawyer, and one of Wisconsin's Top 100 Trial Lawyers.

— WWW.GROTHLAWFIRM.COM —

Thomas J. Giordano, Jr. began as a workers' compensation attorney, eventually becoming a founding partner of Pennsylvania's largest disability law firm, Pond Lehocky Giordano, LLP. With a background in advocating for the injured, he oversees firm operations, emphasizes client service, and maintains a supportive firm culture.

His passion for helping people and his partnership with industry leaders have driven the firm's growth and impact. Giordano's commitment lies in ensuring justice for the injured and disabled for generations to come.

— WWW.PONDLEHOCKY.COM —

Bill Biggs brings over 15 years of executive experience in personal injury law firms, holding CEO and COO roles that spotlight his innovative approach to law firm leadership and operations. His transformative strategies in culture and leadership development have reshaped personal injury firms across the nation, making him a pivotal figure in law firm consulting. Bill's insights have assisted over 100 top U.S. firms to achieve unprecedented growth, and as a speaker and mastermind leader, he has profoundly influenced thousands of law firm leaders with his dynamic seminars and podcasts.

Currently, Bill serves as the Executive Director of Garces, Grabler, LeBrocq, and President of Fireproof Masterminds. He is also the founder of the Master Plan & Law Firm Leadership Summit and hosts the Transforming The Culture of Law Podcast. Beyond the legal arena, he presides over Biggs & Associates, offering brand and messaging strategies to high-profile sports professionals and teams, including Heisman Trophy winners and NFL Hall of Famers. A distinguished graduate of Texas A&M University with a M.Ed in Educational Psychology and an executive alumnus of Harvard Business School's CORe program, Bill lives in College Station, Texas, with his beautiful wife, two sons, and a herd of dogs.

— WWW.VISTACT.COM —

Tim McKey is the co-founder of Vista Consulting, a firm dedicated to helping plaintiff law firms achieve their potential. With decades of experience in accounting and consulting, Tim is skilled at assisting Vista clients with developing a realistic vision for their firms' future and creating a strategic plan to achieve it.

In addition to his work at Vista, Tim is the managing partner of The McKey Business Group (MBG) CPAs. Tim's ability to mentor business owners, gently push them to new levels of thinking, and provide creative perspectives contributes to Vista's success in developing a team of consultants who take a comprehensive approach to working with their clients to achieve enhanced profitability and having fun doing it.

— WWW.VISTACT.COM —

Ken Hardison has over 30 years of legal experience and has personally grown and sold two seven-figure law firms. With a passion and deep understanding of grassroots and cutting-edge online legal marketing strategies, Ken is committed to helping lawyers experience greater financial success, freedom, and personal satisfaction by building an ethical and exceptional law practice.

Ken guides lawyers through the steps needed to build the law practice many have only dreamed possible. Ken is the founder of PILMMA: Powerful Innovative Legal Marketing and Management Association, which is dedicated to helping lawyers learn critical strategies for success.

Ken is the host of the Grow Your Law Firm podcast and author of the best-selling books *Systematic Marketing* and *Under Promise, Over Deliver*.

— WWW.KENHARDISON.COM —

Michael Mogill is the Founder & CEO of Crisp, the nation's number one law firm growth company, and author of *The Game Changing Attorney*. He's also the host of The Game Changing Attorney Podcast and founder of the Game Changers Summit, Earth's largest law firm growth conference. He's helped thousands of attorneys—from solo and small firms to large practices—differentiate themselves from competitors and earn millions in new revenue.

A sought-after speaker, Michael often presents at national conferences on innovative ways to create exponential business growth. His advice has been featured in Forbes, Inc., Avvo, ABA Journal, The Trial Lawyer, Huffington Post, and The Wall Street Journal.

— WWW.MICHAELMOGILL.COM —

Michael Alder is the owner and Senior Trial Attorney at AlderLaw, a prominent Los Angeles firm specializing in personal injury and employment litigation. Renowned as one of California's top trial attorneys, Michael is dedicated to representing underdog clients and has secured over $2.1 billion in verdicts and settlements. His notable achievements include a $60 million verdict in City of Modesto v. Dow Chemical.

With 29+ years in litigation, Michael has received numerous accolades, including CAALA's Trial Lawyer of the Year and the California State Bar's Clay Award. He is an active member of the American Board of Trial Advocates (ABOTA) and serves on its Executive Committee.

— WWW.ALDERLAW.COM —

Chapter 3

WHY CHOOSE A CHIROPRACTOR

"Chiropractic treatment is not merely about addressing the symptoms but about understanding and treating the root cause of pain."

— MARCO LOPEZ, DC

CHIROPRACTIC CARE is an option for anyone dealing with a personal injury, particularly those who are suffering from musculoskeletal issues. Going to a chiropractor is one of the smartest things anyone with a personal injury can do. That's why I interviewed multiple chiropractors about why working with them can be beneficial both for your health, and for your personal injury case. Many people who get into car collisions or have incidents at work might not know that going to a chiropractor is not only an option, but it also allows victims to take a holistic approach to their healing.

While going to a doctor is an important part of any personal injury case, having a chiropractor on your care team increases the frequency of patient interactions, especially in the initial stages of treatment. Unfortunately, many people have outdated perceptions of chiropractors, even though they are well-educated and licensed professionals who undergo rigorous training and examination processes like those required for medical doctors. As Blessen Abraham, DC points out, "Many people still hold misconceptions about chiropractors, dismissing us as quacks or not real doctors. However, we are licensed professionals in every state, recognized as physicians capable of diagnosing and treating various conditions." It's vital to understand the role chiropractors play in healthcare, especially considering they can conduct thorough evaluations and coordinate comprehensive treatment plans without the need for invasive procedures.

Marco Lopez, DC similarly highlights that chiropractors can diagnose conditions, direct care, and make referrals to specialists when necessary: "Chiropractors go through a rigorous screening process, including a national board exam that is independent of graduation. This is similar to the exams physicians must take, followed by an independent registration process with the state." Dr. Lopez notes, "We do have physician status, which means we're able to diagnose and direct care. For example, unlike acupuncturists or physical therapists, who typically cannot order imaging or make certain referrals, I have the authority to refer someone to a neurosurgeon, neurologist, orthopedist, rheumatologist, or for an ultrasound, MRI, or CT scan." Both Dr. Lopez and Dr. Abraham agree the main difference between chiropractors and medical doctors is chiropractors don't prescribe medication. Instead, chiropractors try to treat the root cause of the problem.

Because chiropractors can diagnose, make referrals, and direct care they are able to ensure that their patients receive comprehensive care that addresses their specific needs. Patients' specific needs are better addressed when they see both chiropractors as well as orthopedic specialists and pain management doctors. Chiropractors can build a relationship with their patients through consistent care because they often see their patients multiple times a week and are able to build a therapeutic relationship with their patients, providing personalized care and responding to individual concerns, which is often not possible in more sporadic medical appointments.

Dr. Lopez finds that seeing his patients frequently, especially in the beginning is essential to creating an impactful relationship with them. "Frequent contact provides numerous opportunities to communicate, get to know the patient, and address their questions." Dr. Lopez expands, "This contrasts with other specialties like pain management, orthopedics, or neurosurgery, where a patient may not see their doctor as regularly—sometimes only monthly or even less frequently. Consequently, we develop a deeper relationship with each individual, acting almost like a counselor in their healing process."

Dr. Abraham likens using a chiropractor as utilizing a tool from your toolbox. He says, "Each medical doctor has their specialty, and these are just some of the tools available. We all work together to help the patient recover more effectively." Different specialists should be used to address different issues. Dr. Abraham points out, "I'm not a surgeon, pain doctor, or orthopedic doctor, so, when necessary, I call on these specialists. We might bring in an orthopedic surgeon for shoulder or joint pain, a pain management doctor to alleviate pain during treatment, or a neurologist to perform nerve tests to ensure there are no underlying nerve issues." Practitioners frequently share insights and approaches to formulate the best treatment plans for each patient. This collaboration extends to integrating chiropractic care with other healthcare services, ensuring that patients receive holistic care that addresses all aspects of a patient's health.

Chiropractic care offers a unique and effective approach to treating injuries and chronic conditions. It combines thorough diagnostic capabilities with a hands-on, drug-free approach to treatment that prioritizes patient comfort and long-term health. If you are recovering from a personal injury incident, chiropractic care provides a valuable and often essential complement to traditional medical treatments. Having a holistic care team is essential to your recovery.

Konstantine Fotiou, DC says he employs a coordinated approach amongst his colleagues. "We collaborate constantly and have practiced side by side for many years. The reason for our long-standing collaboration is that we all agree on treatment plans. Sometimes, we also interchange roles within the offices. Over the years, we've borrowed knowledge from each other, and our treatment plan is a composite of insights from each doctor. This collaboration has enabled us to develop an optimal treatment plan tailored to each individual patient."

Michael Chillemi, DC, functional medicine, pain management, and alternative medicine chiropractic expert, agrees that a holistic approach to treating patients is a must, especially in personal injury cases. He argues, "This method helps us to accurately identify the problem and determine the best course of action for each patient." No two patients are alike, and they shouldn't be treated as such. By collaborating with different doctors, physical therapists, and chiropractors, a personal injury victim should be getting the best care possible. As Dr. Fotiou points out, "You cannot treat every patient the same. You want to find a well-versed chiropractic facility that can see all ranges of body types, ages, and injuries."

Dr. Abraham concurs that chiropractic care treats the body holistically and aims to find the problem instead of simply treating its symptoms. He explains, "This means we do not inject or dispense medications. Instead, we use tools such as ultrasound or e-stim machines among various others to help the body heal itself at its own pace or an accelerated one. This approach can prevent the masking of issues that often occurs with medication, and instead, focuses on healing the underlying problem."

This holistic approach includes patients being involved in their own care and understanding their injuries. This can be achieved simply by sharing scans with patients. As Kenneth Ermann, DC, sports medicine and chiropractic health expert notes, "Patients are very attentive and appreciative when I display their scans. Often, even surgeons do not display these scans. Sometimes, doctors don't even review the images themselves; they only read the reports. Therefore, patients are sometimes reassured simply by the fact that we are actually reviewing the images together, rather than just relaying the words or reading from the reports." This kind of investment in patients reassures them they are being listened to while also having someone explain to them what is going on with their body.

Having a chiropractor who can explain things in plain terms is not only beneficial for the patients, but also for testifying in court. Dr. Ermann explains, "When you're in court, the jury needs to hear it in everyday language, not medical terms. Doctors use medical terms every day, but people don't understand those terms. Using medical jargon will not clarify much for a jury, nor will it help a patient understand their treatment protocols. Therefore, speaking plainly is crucial, as is taking the time to ensure they comprehend the explanations provided."

Many people believe insurance companies don't care about victims, they care about making money. Dr. Ermann learned that the difficult way, after being in a bus crash. As he recalls, "This experience was eye-opening. I began to deeply understand the complexities of the insurance industry and how their perspectives could lead patients to abandon their treatment plans out of frustration, suffering persistent pain and permanent injuries. Their quick dismissals based on superficial assessments could result in patients living with significant physical discomfort and diminished quality of life."

That's why having the right chiropractor on your care team is essential to your case's defense. Chiropractors and other specialists become expert witnesses in your case. Dr. Ermann explains, "A testifying expert must first and foremost possess the credibility to clearly communicate with the jury about the events in question. This role involves a bit of storytelling—you must narrate the patient's story, which starts with a trauma. Describe how the trauma occurred, detail the mechanism of the injury, and explain the interactions, such as how two vehicles collided or how a slip and fall happened. Illustrate how these incidents twisted the person's body, leading to disruptions in muscles, tendons, or discs, and how these injuries resulted in pain and dysfunction. It is crucial to establish causality, showing that the cause was the motor vehicle collision or the slip and fall, not years of a sedentary lifestyle or active parenting."

Dr. Fotiou says because he wants the best outcome for his patients he takes testifying very seriously. "I understand that injuries from auto collisions can haunt patients for the rest of their lives, and this needs to be clearly explained in court. We've had great success in helping patients by establishing an objective basis for their injuries, testifying in court, and presenting the extent of their injuries so everyone can understand the severity." Dr. Fotiou stresses the importance of this role, as chiropractors can provide crucial testimony that supports patients' claims about the extent and impact of their injuries. Chiropractors are skilled in differentiating between injuries caused by trauma, such as those from car wrecks, and degenerative conditions like arthritis. This expertise is critical in formulating an effective treatment plan and in legal contexts, where establishing the cause of the injury is necessary.

Dr. Ermann treats his patients with the following eight-word philosophy: "The needs of the patient always come first. If you aren't putting the patient first, you aren't doing your job as a chiropractor." He explains, "The focus is solely on discovering the patient's needs, their goals—whether they want to return to the exact condition they were in before the injury or just well enough to return to work the next day. Once we understand their goals, we can develop a treatment plan to achieve them."

The benefits of chiropractic care in the realm of personal injury cannot be overstated. Chiropractic care goes beyond mere symptom management; it addresses the root causes of pain and dysfunction through a holistic, hands-on approach. This form of care is pivotal not only for alleviating immediate discomfort but also for facilitating long-term recovery and functionality.

The unique perspective and expertise of chiropractors make them invaluable, especially in legal contexts where understanding the extent and cause of injuries is essential. Their contributions can significantly influence the outcomes of personal injury cases by providing clear, objective, and detailed explanations of injuries and their implications.

Embracing chiropractic care offers patients a proactive pathway towards recovery, emphasizing patient empowerment, ongoing support, and a deeper understanding of their physical condition. It ensures that each patient is seen, heard, and given the best possible care and attention, regardless of the circumstances leading to their injury.

TAKEAWAYS FROM THIS CHAPTER

1. **Professional Recognition and Licensing:** Chiropractors are licensed professionals in every state, recognized as capable of diagnosing and treating various conditions. This professional status is crucial, especially as many still harbor misconceptions about the legitimacy and scope of chiropractic care.

2. **Rigorous Training and Examination:** Like medical doctors, chiropractors undergo a rigorous education and screening process, including a national board exam that is independent of their graduation, followed by an independent registration process with the state. This extensive training ensures that chiropractors are well-equipped to handle a wide range of health issues.

3. **Holistic and Non-Invasive Approach:** Chiropractic care is comprehensive and coordinated, focusing on diagnosing and treating the root causes of pain and dysfunction without the use of invasive procedures or medications. This approach not only treats the symptoms but also addresses the underlying causes of discomfort.

4. **Authority to Refer and Direct Care:** Chiropractors have the authority to diagnose conditions and refer patients to specialists such as neurosurgeons, orthopedists, and rheumatologists, which is often necessary for comprehensive treatment. This capability ensures that patients receive holistic care that covers all aspects of their health needs.

5. **Patient-Centered Care:** Chiropractic care emphasizes frequent and thorough patient interactions, which allows chiropractors to build strong, therapeutic relationships with their patients. This approach is particularly beneficial in the initial stages of treatment following an injury, as it allows for continuous assessment and adjustment of treatment plans based on the patient's recovery progress.

Blessen Abraham, DC, first started practicing with his father in Philadelphia, Pennsylvania. He then branched out to the New Brunswick, New Jersey, area, where he continues to practice.

Dr. Abraham likes to motivate his patients to take an active role in their health. His personal mission is to help educate, enlighten, and learn from every person that walks into his practice. Being all-inclusive, unbiased, and open-minded to patients' needs. He grew up with his father's chiropractic practice and practiced with his father until he retired.

— WWW.BRUNSWICKPTCENTER.COM —

Marco A. Lopez, DC is a highly regarded chiropractor specializing in spinal disorders, recognized as a Top Doctor in 2014. Dr. Lopez is a dedicated primary spine care physician who provides non-surgical, non-invasive treatments tailored to each patient's needs. His approach emphasizes early and conservative care, avoiding surgical interventions whenever possible. He collaborates with a multidisciplinary team to ensure comprehensive care for spine-related conditions. In addition to his chiropractic practice, Dr. Lopez is trained in electrodiagnostics and conducts on-site and off-site testing for physicians in the New York Metropolitan area. Dr. Lopez is committed to helping patients return to their daily lives swiftly and effectively.

— WWW.NJSPINEDOC.COM —

Konstantine Fotiou, DC, is the clinic director and sole proprietor of First Care. Dr. Fotiou is proficient in many chiropractic techniques and utilizes updated physiotherapy to address the individual needs of every patient. He has testified in the courts numerous times as an expert witness, attesting to his patients' injuries.

Dr. Fotiou has been actively treating patients for almost 20 years. He has treated numerous patients with conditions ranging from arthritis, maintenance care, and trauma-induced injuries arising from auto collisions, sports injuries, and work-related injuries.

— WWW.FIRSTCARECHIRONJ.COM —

Michael Chillemi, DC, is licensed in New Jersey, New York, Florida, and Pennsylvania. He is certified by the National Board of Chiropractic and the American International Sports Association. He is also certified in Flexion Distraction, Functional Capacity Evaluations, and Cardiac Resuscitation. He co-authored *The Complete Herbal Guide: A Natural Approach to Healing the Body.*

Dr. Chillemi maximizes his treatments with postural, strengthening, and stretching exercises. He has enjoyed a high success rate with stabilizing displaced spinal discs. He offers extensive care and treatment for injuries that range from acute to chronic, cervical and lumbar disc conditions, sports-related injuries, shoulder dysfunction, knee dysfunction, and rehabilitation of the functional body. He has also adopted and mastered cutting-edge examination methodology and developed a system of X-ray analysis to screen out potential risks.

— WWW.HEALTHSPINEWELLNESS.COM —

Kenneth Ermann, DC, is a highly esteemed Sports Medicine and Chiropractic expert with over 35 years of experience in North Jersey. Known for his extensive credentials, Dr. Ken has served as the Official Team Chiropractor for the New York Giants for over two decades, providing care to NFL athletes on and off the field, including at multiple Super Bowls. His expertise extends to the NBA, serving as the Official Team Chiropractor for the New Jersey Nets. His clientele includes MVPs from the NFL, MLB, NHL, and NBA, CEOs, and celebrities from various industries.

As a survivor of a serious personal injury himself, Dr. Ken brings a unique perspective to his practice, offering compassionate and knowledgeable care. He is also a seasoned expert witness, providing critical testimony in legal proceedings across the United States, including Texas, Idaho, New York, Minnesota, Florida, Maryland, Georgia, Colorado, and New Jersey.

— WWW.DRKENERMANN.COM —

Chapter 4

THE ROLE OF THE PAIN MANAGEMENT DOCTOR

"As a board-certified doctor, it is my job to advocate for the patient and do everything I can to offer the necessary therapy."

— DIDIER DEMESMIN, MD, MBA

NAVIGATING THE AFTERMATH of a personal injury, especially one stemming from a motor vehicle collision, is complex and often overwhelming. The convergence of medical care, legal proceedings, and insurance claims can be daunting for anyone. Having a dedicated pain management doctor can significantly improve the outcome for patients, offering both immediate relief and long-term support. This chapter delves into the importance of having a pain management doctor in the context of personal injury cases.

Pain management doctors specialize in the evaluation, diagnosis, and treatment of pain. Their expertise is vital in the context of personal injuries, as they provide comprehensive care that addresses both the immediate and long-term effects of injuries. Douglas J. Spiel, M.D., board certified radiologist, emphasizes the uniqueness of personal injury cases, particularly those resulting from motor vehicle collisions. In New Jersey, for example, personal injury benefits often take precedence over medical insurance, ensuring that victims receive the necessary care without financial barriers. Spiel notes, "Personal injury is its own niche. If you're involved in a motor vehicle crash, at least in New Jersey, you have some kind of personal injury benefits, which usually take precedence over your medical insurance." This prioritization underscores the importance of timely and specialized care for those affected.

Seeing a doctor, specifically a pain management doctor, is crucial after an injury because it is very common for insurance companies to conclude that there is no injury. Even when someone has horrific injuries the insurance company will try to assert that the person is healthy and uninjured. They often claim there is no permanent injury and no causal relationship with the incident. In court, the insurance companies argue that the injuries are degenerative in nature as opposed to traumatic. Ruby Kim, M.D., Interventional Pain Management Specialist, explains why the first thing you should do after an incident is call a doctor: "The first person you should call is a doctor, ideally a pain management doctor. Doctors can diagnose patients from head to toe, identify any major medical issues, prescribe medications, and help you get time off work to recover." Dr. Kim notes, "We can mobilize you quickly and provide access to a variety of specialties right away."

When a patient first visits a pain management doctor after an injury, a detailed history is taken. This history is crucial in understanding the extent of the injury and any pre-existing conditions. Dr. Spiel emphasizes the importance of this process. "If you come into our office and say, 'Hey,

THE ROLE OF THE PAIN MANAGEMENT DOCTOR

doc, my back hurts," we take a history and ask questions like, "Have you ever had back pain before? Have you ever had treatment for back pain? Have you ever had an MRI of your lower back? Has your prior injury ever required imaging, EMG, NCV studies, treatments with physiatrists, chiropractors, or epidurals?" One of the key diagnostic tools used by pain management doctors is the MRI. Dr. Spiel highlights the significance of comparing pre and post-injury MRIs to identify acute changes. He explains, "Occasionally, there will be changes between an MRI done before the injury and one done afterward. I look at the injury, compare it to their signs and symptoms, and most importantly, determine if there was a significant physiological change and if there is some anatomical change." This comparison helps in pinpointing the exact cause of pain and formulating an effective treatment plan, as well as proving that the pain started after the patient's incident.

That history is powerful. If the patient has a prior MRI a pain management doctor can compare it to their new one. Dr. Spiel states, "Sometimes on an MRI, I'll see specific sentinel findings that are very indicative of an acute injury. I'll see inflammatory changes in a bone, tears in the disc, and other things explained by acute changes. We can identify findings that are acute or subacute." This is especially important for a personal injury claim because it can prove the pain the patient is experiencing is real and directly associated to the incident they were in.

As noted, one of the significant challenges in pain management is dealing with insurance companies. Didier Demesmin, M.D., MBA, highlights the difficulties faced when insurance companies deny necessary procedures. He explains, "Often, the way we want to treat a patient conflicts with the insurance company's guidelines, making us jump through hoops. For example, if a patient has a disc herniation compressing a nerve, causing back pain that radiates down the legs, and we have objective evidence from an MRI showing this, we might want to pre-certify an epidural steroid injection. This means seeking the insurance company's permission to perform the injection. Sometimes, the insurance company refuses for one reason or another, which can be perplexing." Despite these challenges, pain management doctors advocate for their patients to ensure they receive the necessary care.

At some point after being injured, you will be asked to have an independent medical evaluation. Many of these doctors are under the umbrella of the insurance company. Dr. Spiel argues, "The insurance company wants to say that all your injuries are pre-existing, not permanent, not serious, and don't merit care, physical therapy, chiropractic manipulation, or any palliative treatments." Being honest with your doctor is one of the smartest things you can do to get the best care possible and to get the best outcome from your personal injury case. As Dr. Spiel notes, "When you come into my office, I want to know your exact history. I want to know what your problems were before and what your problems are now. Don't hide things. If you have a drug history, smoking history, or something else you want to share with me, that's important for how I treat you." If you aren't honest about your medical history, it endangers your care and makes it harder for doctors to be on your side.

Over the past decade, pain management has seen remarkable advancements, which helps provide evidence for personal injury cases. Traditionally, anatomical evaluations were used to diagnose pain, but modern approaches now incorporate advanced imaging technologies. Dr. Spiel points out, "As the world has changed over the last decade, we're seeing some remarkable developments. There's an expansion of

THE ROLE OF THE PAIN MANAGEMENT DOCTOR

many modalities we used to use. We previously relied on anatomical evaluations, and then figured out physiologically what hurts. Now, we have more advanced imaging that looks at physiology, allowing us to see what actually hurts." The integration of artificial intelligence in radiology has further enhanced the accuracy of diagnoses, providing clearer insights into conditions such as herniations and making it easier for your doctor to prove that the pain you are experiencing is a direct result of your injury.

It is important for patients to follow the care path suggested by insurance companies. As Dr. Spiel notes, "The insurance companies want you to go through physical therapy or chiropractic care unless you have an indication that you absolutely need imaging first. So, you'll go through your six weeks of treatment, we'll reevaluate you, and decide what to do next." If there is no improvement after doing physical therapy and chiropractic care, pain management doctors can determine something is structurally and physiologically unsound and they need to treat it. Dr. Spiel explains, "We go through the pre-certification process, and the insurance company may come back and deny it for various reasons. We might submit it again with additional data, either from the literature or my personal experience, and then decide whether to wait or go forward. If a doctor decides to go forward, it means two things: we believe you're really hurt, and we believe we can make you better."

Because each patient is different and each injury is different, pain management doctors tailor treatment plans based on the specific needs of each patient. This personalized approach ensures that patients receive the most appropriate care for their condition. Dr. Kim, a physiatrist, underscores the importance of a comprehensive evaluation and swift action in managing pain: "Once you see your doctor, we might recommend seeing a physical therapist, chiropractor, or acupuncturist."

Collaborative care goes beyond meeting with chiropractors and physical therapists, however. Dr. Demesmin emphasizes the importance of a team approach in managing complex cases. "I see medicine as a team effort. If a patient presents with trauma to the lumbar spine and has other health conditions, such as poorly controlled diabetes or high blood pressure, we need to ensure the patient is stable enough to undergo procedures like an epidural, nerve block, or surgery." This collaboration ensures that all aspects of a patient's health are considered, leading to better outcomes.

Dr. Spiel agrees that it is important for patients to be honest about the entirety of their medical past and shares a story that highlights this importance. "I had a patient in the OR the other day who didn't want to tell the anesthesiologist about the opioids she was taking. That's not right. It endangers your care and makes it harder for us to be on your side." So, having a full medical history is crucial in making sure personal injury victims are getting the best care possible.

Because personal injury cases often result in chronic pain, requiring long-term management and rehabilitation, pain management doctors play a crucial role in guiding patients through this process. Dr. Demesmin discusses the importance of ongoing care: "Even during my interventions and after surgery, patients still need chiropractic treatment and physical therapy to rehabilitate their muscles. When a disc injury occurs, two things happen: the nerve gets compressed, causing pain, and the back muscles become atrophied and weaker." By providing comprehensive care, pain management doctors help patients regain strength and improve their quality of life.

Dr. Demesmin argues that many conditions can become permanent. For example, he says, "After disc herniation, no matter how many surgical procedures or injections you undergo, the disc will never function the same way as it did normally. Once you have an injury to a disc, even if you can fix it with a discectomy to reduce symptoms, the patient will lose some function of that disc. Instead of working at 100%, it might function at 75% or even 50%. The patient may experience less pain and discomfort over time, but there will always be some limitation in their functional ability."

If a patient can never return to 100% function, then they have a permanent injury. As Dr. Demesmin points out, "Despite having many great surgeons in our community who do excellent work, patients may become a bit more comfortable and have improved quality of life, but they will never be 100% the same. They will have some limitations in the work they can do and the types of activities they can engage in. This is what makes it a permanent condition."

Dr. Kim explains pain management is not solely about addressing physical symptoms. It also involves understanding the psychological impact of pain. There is a close relationship between pain and psychological factors, particularly post-injury. She explains, "Pain is highly subjective. People may report experiencing severe pain, so I observe them during the exam. The exam seems benign, just walking or sitting down, and simply asking them to get up on the exam table. You see different body parts moving, how they move, and which joints are involved. This allows you to see how patients move." By considering these aspects, pain management doctors can develop more effective treatment plans.

This is why in personal injury cases, the collaboration between medical and legal professionals is essential. Dr. Spiel describes the relationship between doctors and attorneys, highlighting the importance of trust and communication. He states, "Liens and letters of protection are situations where you need to trust your attorney, and your attorney needs to trust your doctor. It's an interesting kind of pyramid trilogy. A letter of protection and a lien essentially mean that you've exhausted your insurance. You may not have any major medical insurance and have limited or exhausted personal injury insurance, but maybe there's some money on the other side that can help pay for your care."

Seeing a pain management doctor after an injury is crucial for several reasons. These specialists provide comprehensive care that addresses both physical and psychological aspects of pain, tailor treatment plans to individual needs, and collaborate with other healthcare professionals to ensure optimal outcomes. Despite the challenges posed by insurance companies, pain management doctors advocate for their patients and work closely with legal professionals to ensure that victims of a personal injury receive the care and compensation they deserve. As the field of pain management continues to evolve, the importance of specialized care in managing pain and improving quality of life becomes increasingly evident. By consulting a pain management doctor, personal injury victims can access the expertise and support needed to navigate their recovery journey, ultimately leading to better health and well-being.

TAKEAWAYS FROM THIS CHAPTER

1. Critical Role of Pain Management Doctors: Pain management doctors are essential after an injury, providing comprehensive care that addresses both immediate and long-term effects of injuries. Their expertise in evaluating, diagnosing, and treating pain ensures that victims receive the necessary care, often prioritized over medical insurance.

2. Importance of Initial Medical Consultation: The first step after a personal injury should be consulting a pain management doctor. They can diagnose the extent of injuries, prescribe medications, and provide access to various specialties. This initial consultation is crucial for understanding the injury's severity and any pre-existing conditions.

3. Challenges with Insurance Companies: Pain management doctors often face obstacles with insurance companies denying necessary procedures. Despite these challenges, they advocate for their patients, ensuring they receive the required care through persistence and thorough documentation.

4. Advanced Diagnostic Tools and Techniques: Modern pain management incorporates advanced imaging technologies and artificial intelligence to diagnose and treat injuries accurately. Comparing pre and post-injury MRIs helps pinpoint the exact cause of pain, providing evidence for personal injury claims.

5. Comprehensive and Collaborative Care: Pain management involves a collaborative approach with other healthcare professionals and legal representatives. This ensures that all aspects of a patient's health are considered, leading to better outcomes. Honesty about medical history and symptoms is vital for effective treatment and support from both medical and legal teams.

Douglas J. Spiel, M.D. is a Board Certified Radiologist and member of the World Institute of Pain with over 20 years of experience in interventional pain. He was the first radiologist in the United States to become a Diplomat of the American Board of Interventional Pain Physicians and currently serves on its executive board.

Dr. Spiel offers surgical and non-surgical treatment options for spine and joint pain, utilizing cutting-edge technologies such as fluoroscopy and ultrasound to diagnose and treat specific pain generators. He is committed to providing the very best in cutting-edge pain management, including emerging treatments, to offer patients previously unavailable options.

— WWW.SPIELMD.COM —

Ruby Kim, M.D. is an interventional pain management specialist who is fellowship-trained and board-certified in physical medicine and rehabilitation. Highly acclaimed within the medical field as one of the best pain management physicians in the Tri-State Area, Dr. Kim is committed to providing excellent quality care to her patients. A native of Livingston, New Jersey, Dr. Kim is now proud to serve her surrounding communities in New Jersey and New York.

Her extensive experience, comprehensive care, and warmth have created a great demand for her services. As a result, Dr. Kim now has offices conveniently located in Fort Lee, NJ and Jersey City, NJ where she diagnoses treatments for a wide spectrum of conditions.

— WWW.PREMIERSPINESPORTS.COM —

Didier Demesmin, M.D., MBA, is a board-certified interventional pain medicine physician and founder of the University Pain and Spine Center, with offices in New Jersey and New York City. He received his medical degree from Rutgers Robert Wood Johnson Medical School. He completed an interventional pain medicine fellowship program at Columbia University Vagelos College of Physicians and Surgeons/Mount Sinai Morningside.

Dr. Demesmin treats a variety of pain syndromes and specializes in minimally invasive procedures such as disc decompression and nerve blocks. He is also involved in clinical research and has lectured internationally.

— WWW.UPMCNJ.COM —

Chapter 5

THE ROLE OF AN ORTHOPEDIST

"The sooner you start your treatments and address the legal aspects of your case, the better your outcome will be."

— DANIEL DORRI, M.D.

ORTHOPEDIC SURGEONS play a critical role in the diagnosis, management, treatment and rehabilitation of patients involved in personal injury cases. Their expertise not only involves surgical interventions but also extends to comprehensive patient assessments, conservative treatment approaches, and multidisciplinary collaboration.

Physical medicine and rehabilitation play a critical role in the recovery of personal injury victims. Understanding the phases of rehabilitation and how to tailor treatments to individual patients is essential. Daniel Dorri, M.D. highlights this importance stating, "Understanding how to rehabilitate patients and the phase of rehabilitation is crucial." Physiatrists are equipped with tools like nerve tests and electromyography (EMG) to identify where nerves and muscles are compromised, allowing for focused treatment.

Additionally, physiatrists treat traumatic brain injuries and spinal cord injuries, ensuring that concussions and other conditions are promptly diagnosed and treated. "During our initial evaluation, we ensure to test for concussions and initiate treatment immediately, as it is crucial to address traumatic brain injuries within 60 days of the injury," Dr. Dorri explains. This early intervention provides a significant advantage that physiatrists have over other specialties.

One of the core principles emphasized by David Porter, M.D. is the necessity of individualized patient assessment. He asserts, "I think when it comes to treating a patient, you have to look at each patient individually. For example, a patient in their mid-20s with a rotator cuff tear could be very different from a patient in their late 50s with a similar tear, or a patient in their early 60s with a new tear. It's important to assess each patient individually." This individualized approach ensures that each patient receives a tailored treatment plan based on their specific condition, age, and overall health status.

Arun Rajaram, M.D. emphasizes the importance of looking at the patient thoroughly. He states, "When I see a patient in the office, I conduct a thorough head-to-toe evaluation. This includes assessing the muscles around the neck and shoulder, evaluating all joints, and examining the lower back, hips, and knees. If the patient displays any concussion symptoms, I connect them with our concussion specialists." This comprehensive assessment helps identify all potential injuries and ensures that no aspect of the patient's condition is overlooked.

Dr. Porter's philosophy extends this to the treatment process itself.

THE ROLE OF AN ORTHOPEDIST

He emphasizes the importance of conservative treatment options before considering surgery. "It's extremely important to go through a process of conservative treatment with many patients. Of course, if a patient needs surgery urgently, we proceed with that. However, we often give patients a chance with conservative treatment options first." This cautious approach helps avoid unnecessary surgical interventions and promotes recovery through less invasive means whenever possible.

Joshua Rovner, M.D. agrees it is important to try conservative treatments first when someone has been injured. He says, "First, they might try medication, such as Tylenol or Advil, and some physical therapy or non-invasive exercises. They might also try chiropractic treatment. If these approaches don't help, they move to a pain management doctor, undergo imaging like an MRI, and possibly receive a cortisone injection." Surgery should be the last option, unless it's an emergency. Dr. Rovner states, "If I see a patient right after their incident, I ensure they receive high-quality physical therapy from skilled therapists tailored to their specific issue. If physical therapy is not effective, I make sure they go to a top-tier MRI facility with high-quality machines to get a thorough and accurate diagnosis."

Most patients initially undergo these conservative treatments such as physical therapy to see how they respond. If there is no improvement within four to six weeks, further action is needed. Symptoms such as sciatica, radiculopathy, or joint damage may require more intensive interventions. "We use various types of injections for different parts of the spine to provide relief and reduce inflammation," Dr. Dorri explains. These injections improve patient function and facilitate a faster rehabilitation process.

Minimally invasive procedures are a cornerstone of modern

orthopedic treatment, aimed at minimizing tissue damage and promoting faster recovery. "The less tissue we destroy, the better the outcome and the faster the recovery," Dr. Dorri emphasizes. This approach allows patients to return to work and society more quickly. The use of scopes, which are roughly the size of a phone camera, facilitates these procedures. "Imagine touching the camera on the back of your iPhone or Samsung; that's the size of the scope used to see inside your body," Dr. Dorri explains.

The benefits of minimally invasive procedures are numerous. Patients often recover quickly and can go home the same day, with reduced pain and suffering post-procedure. This makes recovery and rehabilitation easier, allowing patients to return to their normal lives sooner. While some cases may require more advanced surgeries, many patients benefit significantly from minimally invasive techniques. "Pain management specialists are particularly skilled in performing these procedures because they understand the anatomy and can navigate it percutaneously, meaning through the skin, without making large incisions," Dr. Dorri adds.

Dr. Rovner also emphasizes the importance of personalized care. "Every patient is different, with unique problems, sizes, heights, weights, and ages. We do not use a cookie-cutter approach; instead, we treat each patient as we would treat a family member or friend." This individualized approach ensures that each patient receives the care and attention they need, tailored to their specific circumstances and needs.

Dr. Rajaram highlights the importance of understanding the mechanism of injury, as it provides valuable insights into potential complications. "The process involves understanding the patient's initial complaints and determining what else could be happening based on the mechanism of injury. Often, due to adrenaline, symptoms can be masked, and the patient may experience pain in various body parts." This awareness allows for a more accurate diagnosis and tailored treatment plan.

Effective communication is another crucial aspect emphasized by Dr. Rajaram. "Communication is crucial. If team members from your office or the legal team are coordinating care for a patient, it's essential to communicate with everyone involved. This helps with scheduling and ensures everyone understands the treatment plan, keeping everyone in the loop." This collaborative approach ensures that all stakeholders are informed and working towards the common goal of optimal patient recovery.

Dr. Rovner and Dr. Porter agree that the role of multidisciplinary collaboration in managing chronic pain is key to helping patients recover. It's important patients see a highly skilled, board-certified doctor who will provide appropriate treatment without over-treating. Dr. Porter states, "Patients with chronic pain are a significant challenge. You could perform a surgery that seems perfect, with a postoperative course as good as it could be, yet the patient still doesn't seem to get better." Dr. Rovner adds, "This collaborative approach with other medical professionals ensures that our patients receive the best possible care from a team that takes pride in their work."

Dr. Porter often refers patients to pain management specialists early in their treatment. "If I'm concerned about a chronic pain issue or patients developing fibromyalgia or chronic pain syndrome, I tend to refer them early in the course to a pain management specialist. These specialists have multiple medications and treatment options to help these patients early on." This collaboration ensures that patients receive the most appropriate and effective treatments, addressing all aspects of their pain and recovery.

Dr. Rovner explains that the integration of advanced technologies in orthopedic surgery significantly enhances patient outcomes. He uses stem cells and 3D printing technology to help his patients. He states, "I use stem cells in my patients by taking bone marrow from the local area of their spine surgery and using their stem cells in their fusions or other surgeries to help them heal better and faster." This innovative approach promotes faster and more effective healing, reducing recovery times and improving patient satisfaction.

Dr. Rovner also highlights the use of 3D-printed titanium cages in spine surgery. "One of the newest advancements in spine surgery is 3D printing. We now have 3D-printed titanium cages, which are designed to mimic the patient's bone structure. This provides a substantial technological advantage." By leveraging these cutting-edge technologies, Dr. Rovner and his team can achieve superior outcomes for their patients.

When it comes to personal injury cases, collaboration with legal professionals is essential. Accurate documentation of the patient's condition and treatment is crucial. Dr. Dorri emphasizes, "It is crucial to document that the patient's injury is due to a specific mechanism. This requires collaboration with lawyers." This meticulous documentation helps in the treatment plan and ensures that the patient's legal case is supported by comprehensive medical evidence.

Training and communication between medical and legal professionals are also vital. Dr. Dorri regularly participates in lawyer conventions and provides training to legal staff to help them understand medical procedures. "This open communication is essential; if we don't talk to each other, we cannot understand what's happening in our respective fields," Dr. Dorri states.

Understanding the language used by both physicians and lawyers is critical. Medical terms need to be translated into legal terms for courtroom presentations. "Knowing this language helps us when preparing documents like narrative reports, peer reviews, or even when testifying," Dr. Dorri explains. This ensures that medical evidence is clearly understood in a legal context.

Choosing the right lawyer and physician is paramount in personal injury cases. Dr. Dorri advises, "Be careful when selecting an attorney." He emphasizes the importance of starting treatments and addressing legal aspects promptly. "Research shows that if you are away from work for three months due to an injury, your chances of returning to your previous level of function are just 5%. If it extends to six months, the chance of returning to normal life drops to less than 1%."

The role of an orthopedic surgeon in personal injury cases is multifaceted, encompassing individualized patient assessments, conservative treatment approaches, advanced technologies, and multidisciplinary collaboration. Orthopedic surgeons play a vital role in managing personal injury cases. Through a combination of conservative treatments, minimally invasive procedures, and advanced interventions, they aim to restore patients to their pre-injury state. Collaboration with legal professionals and meticulous documentation are crucial to ensuring that patients receive the care and compensation they deserve. By understanding the nuances of both medical and legal language, orthopedists can effectively advocate for their patients, providing comprehensive care and support throughout the recovery process.

TAKEAWAYS FROM THIS CHAPTER

1. Comprehensive Patient Assessments: Orthopedic surgeons emphasize individualized patient assessments to tailor treatment plans based on specific conditions, ages, and health statuses. Thorough evaluations are essential to identify all potential injuries and ensure that no aspect of the patient's condition is overlooked.

2. Conservative Treatment Approaches: Before considering surgery, conservative treatment options such as physical therapy, medications, and non-invasive exercises are prioritized. This cautious approach helps avoid unnecessary surgical interventions and promotes recovery through less invasive means.

3. Minimally Invasive Procedures: Minimally invasive techniques are a cornerstone of modern orthopedic treatment, aimed at minimizing tissue damage and promoting faster recovery. The use of advanced technologies, like scopes and 3D-printed titanium cages, enhances patient outcomes and allows for quicker return to normal activities.

4. Multidisciplinary Collaboration: Effective communication and collaboration among healthcare providers, including pain management specialists, physiatrists, and legal professionals, are crucial. This collaborative approach ensures comprehensive care, addressing all aspects of the patient's pain and recovery, and supporting the legal case with detailed documentation.

5. Importance of Early Intervention and Documentation: Early intervention and meticulous documentation are vital in managing personal injury cases. Accurate documentation of injuries, treatments, and patient progress supports both medical and legal aspects, ensuring patients receive appropriate care and compensation. Collaboration with lawyers and understanding the language used in legal contexts further enhance the effectiveness of treatment and advocacy for patients.

Daniel Dorri, M.D., is a board-certified, fellowship-trained physician specializing in pain management, physical medicine, and sports medicine. He is renowned for his minimally invasive spine and orthopedic pain management expertise and performs advanced ultrasound-guided procedures.

Dr. Dorri's medical journey began in Iran, where he graduated from Shahid Beheshti University and served as a sports medicine physician, including roles as an Olympic team doctor. After relocating to the U.S., he completed his surgical training at Montefiore Hospital and his physical medicine and rehabilitation training at New York Medical College.

— WWW.HUDSONREGIONALHOSPITAL.COM —

David Porter, M.D., is a board-certified Orthopedic Surgeon specializing in sports medicine issues such as knee and shoulder pain. He earned his medical degree at Rutgers Medical School and became the Chief Resident in Orthopaedic Surgery at Lenox Hill Hospital in New York City. Dr. Porter expanded his knowledge in the field further by completing a fellowship in Sports Medicine at Miami Orthopedics and Sports Medicine Institute.

During his fellowship, Dr. Porter focused on minimally invasive arthroscopic techniques for treating sports-related injuries. He has worked with numerous athletic teams, notably the NHL Florida Panthers, the NBA Heat, and the NFL Miami Dolphins. Dr. Porter now practices in Northern New Jersey and operates at multiple hospitals.

— WWW.NEWJERSEYSPINESURGEON.COM —

THE ROLE OF AN ORTHOPEDIST

Arun Rajaram, M.D., is a native of New Jersey who was born and raised in Morris County, New Jersey. He completed his orthopedic surgery residency at Yale University and his orthopedic sports medicine fellowship through the Baylor College of Medicine at the Texas Medical Center, the largest medical center in the world. As an orthopedic surgeon specializing in sports medicine and arthroscopic surgery, Dr. Rajaram uses the most advanced techniques available to surgeons.

During his fellowship, Dr. Rajaram gained phenomenal experience as an assistant team physician for multiple professional teams, including the Houston Texans, Rockets, Astros, and Dynamo.

— WWW.ALLIANCEORTHO.COM —

Joshua Rovner, M.D., earned his medical degree from New York Downstate College of Medicine. He then completed a residency in orthopedic surgery at Albert Einstein College of Medicine and a spine fellowship at Twin Cities Spine Center in Minneapolis. He is recognized for his expertise in minimally invasive techniques and is board-certified in orthopedic surgery with a specialization in spine surgery.

Practicing in Englewood, New Jersey, Dr. Rovner is one of the few spine specialists in the state qualified to perform robotic procedures, enhancing precision and patient outcomes. His advanced methods result in less blood loss, reduced risks, faster recovery, and less post-operative pain. Known for his compassionate approach, Dr. Rovner is dedicated to easing patients' fears and ensuring they feel confident in his care.

— WWW.NEWJERSEYSPINESURGEON.COM —

Chapter 6

WHEN TO SEE A NEUROLOGIST

"Helping people who can't use their legs walk again, albeit with recuperation time, is just an amazing feeling."

— HARSHIPAL SINGH, MD

NEUROLOGISTS PLAY A CRITICAL ROLE in helping those who have a brain or spine injury as a result from a personal injury case. When it comes to injuries, especially those involving the brain and spine, the immediate steps you take can significantly influence your recovery trajectory. This chapter examines the critical nature of timely medical intervention following any form of personal injury that may involve the nervous system. It will also delve into advancements made in spine and brain surgery.

Gregory Lawler, D.O. explains that personal injury cases involving spinal cord injuries usually stem from car collisions, slip and falls, construction, and work-related injuries. He says, "The biggest challenge is dealing with the patient's frustration and pain and navigating the complex healthcare system to provide timely and appropriate care."

Treatments for spine and brain injuries should start right away and often involve a multidisciplinary approach. Dr. Lawler emphasizes the importance of early intervention, stating, "There's no time like the present in terms of a brain injury," and stresses why having a multidisciplinary approach is vital in cases such as these. "You can't have every patient undergo the same treatment algorithm when they have an injury. It's a case-by-case basis."

Nirav K. Shah, MD, FANNS, FACS, explains, "Brain injuries encompass a wide spectrum, including surgical cases where the damage is apparent, such as when someone suffers a direct blow to the head that leads to bleeding." In these scenarios, emergency surgery might be required to alleviate bleeding and reduce intracranial pressure. These are categorized as catastrophic injuries, demanding immediate and aggressive treatment.

On the other end of the spectrum lie concussions, which are considered non-surgical but can still have profound impacts. "Neurosurgeons frequently manage non-surgical issues," Dr. Shah notes, highlighting the versatility required in this field. This statement underscores that neurosurgeons are comprehensive caretakers of brain health, capable of managing conditions that do not necessitate surgery.

Additionally, spinal cord injuries, which affect the neck and mid-back, present their own set of challenges. Dr. Lawler notes, "When someone has a spinal cord issue, it often involves weakness or sensory loss from compression of the spinal cord, which may require surgery, aggressive physical therapy, or pain management." Evaluating the patient quickly and accurately is crucial, often involving MRI and CAT scans, followed by a clinical correlation where the neurosurgeon interprets the results in the context of the patient's condition.

When it comes to diagnosing and treating spine injuries, Edward Scheid, MD also emphasized a personalized and multidisciplinary approach. "You can't just look at an MRI and say that there is a herniated disc, and the patient needs surgery. You must interview the patient and get a very detailed history. Understanding the incident and the patient's experience is crucial."

Dr. Shah emphasizes how treatment for brain injuries should be highly personalized and explains how the range of interventions starts with conservative management, such as rest and medication, and ranges to more active treatments like surgery or specialized therapies depending on the severity of the injury. "Treatment is tailored on a case-by-case basis," he asserts, highlighting the need for personalized care plans based on each patient's unique circumstances.

Dr. Scheid highlights the importance of a thorough physical examination and diagnostic imaging to form an accurate treatment plan. "You need to know the details, such as the speed of the vehicles involved and whether the patient was wearing a seatbelt. During the physical examination I identify which nerve roots are affected and correlate that with the MRI findings."

In developing a treatment plan, Dr. Scheid emphasizes understanding the patient's history and injury mechanisms. Initial steps often include ordering imaging studies and starting physical therapy or chiropractic care. Electromyography (EMG) is another tool used to assess nerve injuries. "EMG monitors the nerves from the fingertips to the cervical spinal cord, giving us valuable information about the degree and location of nerve injuries," Dr. Scheid explains.

Harshipal Singh, MD places a strong emphasis on personalized patient care as well. He believes that understanding each patient's unique circumstances and medical history is crucial for successful treatment. "Every patient is different," Dr. Singh notes. "We need to tailor our approach to meet their specific needs. This includes taking the time to listen to their concerns, thoroughly reviewing their medical history, and developing a treatment plan that is best suited to their condition."

Dr. Shah stresses the urgency of seeing a neurologist or neurosurgeon immediately after an injury. "First and foremost, we strive to see patients with cognitive issues as quickly as possible. There's no time like the present when it comes to brain injuries," he states. This urgency is crucial to ensure that patients receive the most accurate assessment and appropriate care swiftly to prevent further complications. "Cognitive ability is the capacity to think, plan, and function in what we often refer to as an executive manner," Dr. Shah explains. Injuries to the brain can disrupt these essential functions, leading to significant challenges in daily life.

Dr. Singh highlights the importance of involving patients in their own care. "Educating patients about their condition and the treatment options available to them is key," he says. "When patients understand their diagnosis and the rationale behind their treatment plan, they are more likely to be engaged and compliant with their care." Dr. Shah agrees, and says "Every time I see a patient, I strive to educate them about their condition. We support this education by reviewing imaging and drawing on our own training and experience regarding these types of injuries."

The relationship between physician and patient is critical in the healing process. Dr. Singh highlights how patient care is deeply personal and why he takes a patient-centered approach. This patient-centered approach involves detailed discussions with patients and their families

WHEN TO SEE A NEUROLOGIST

about treatment options and expected outcomes. Dr. Singh encourages family members to participate in consultations to ensure everyone understands the treatment plan. "Part of healing is not just the patient itself, it's the patient's family. It's also the patient and their family understanding what is involved," he explained.

Dr. Singh emphasized the importance of understanding the severity of spinal injuries when treating personal injury cases. "If someone is in a collision or fall, and they have weakness or inability to move or paralysis, that's a life-threatening emergency," he stated. In such cases, immediate surgical intervention is crucial to stabilize the spine and decompress the spinal cord, which can significantly impact the patient's long-term recovery prospects.

However, not all spinal injuries require surgery. "A lot of spinal injuries can be treated with injections, therapy, and time," Dr. Singh noted. Conservative treatments are often effective for non-critical injuries, highlighting the importance of personalized care plans. For patients with non-operative indications, interventions such as steroid injections, physical therapy, and other non-surgical treatments can provide substantial relief.

Dr. Scheid agrees that conservative treatments should be tried first and believes surgery should always be a last resort. "Patients offered surgery by me have usually exhausted every other option, such as physical therapy, chiropractic manipulation, and steroid injections. However, if a patient has a neurologic deficit, like weakness or numbness in an arm or leg, or bowel and bladder problems from back or neck issues, surgery may be necessary right away." Neurological deficits require prompt surgical intervention to prevent permanent damage. "Time is of the essence with nerve injuries. Delaying surgery could lead to worse neurological outcomes," Dr. Scheid explains.

When surgery becomes unavoidable, Dr. Scheid utilizes advanced techniques to ensure patient safety. "Technology has advanced significantly over the last 10 to 15 years. We used to perform open spine surgeries with large incisions and extensive dissections. Now, we treat patients with minimally invasive approaches—smaller incisions, minimal blood loss, quicker surgeries, and faster recoveries."

Dr. Scheid's research focuses on improving the safety of these procedures through neuro-monitoring, which allows real-time monitoring of nerves and the spinal cord during surgery. "This ensures that whatever we're doing to fix the problem isn't causing any damage, making surgery much safer." Minimally invasive techniques have revolutionized spinal surgery. "Even procedures like laminectomies can now be done through minimal approaches," Dr. Scheid says. "It's like building a ship inside a bottle—you go in through a small opening but have full access to the necessary areas." The benefits of minimally invasive surgery extend beyond smaller scars. "The biggest advantage is the recovery. Patients experience less pain and can return to normal activities much quicker. There's also less scarring in the muscles, which means less stiffness and prolonged pain over time," Dr. Scheid explains.

As noted, in addition to helping people with spine injuries, neurologists also help people with brain injuries, especially concussions. Brain injuries in personal injury cases can vary greatly in severity and impact. Dr. Lawler explained, "Brain injuries have a wide spectrum, from surgical cases where someone has a direct blow to the head and develops bleeding, to non-surgical cases like concussions." Surgical cases often involve immediate intervention to evacuate bleeding and reduce pressure in the brain, which can be lifesaving. On the other hand, concussions, while not requiring surgery, still demand expert care to manage symptoms and prevent long-term damage.

The cognitive abilities of a person suffering from a traumatic brain injury can be significantly affected. Dr. Lawler described cognitive ability as "The ability to think and plan and function in what we call an executive manner." He likened the brain to a cell phone: "If you drop your cell phone and it looks fine but doesn't work properly, that's similar to what happens in the brain at a cellular level." This disconnection can lead to difficulties in thinking, memory, speech, and emotional regulation, profoundly impacting the patient's daily life.

One of the misconceptions people have about brain and spinal cord injuries is the wide spectrum of symptoms and the severity of the injuries. Dr. Lawler highlighted the need for public awareness, stating, "Because there's such a wide spectrum of symptoms, people might not recognize the severity of a spinal cord injury even though it is significant." It's vital to see a neurologist after a spine or brain injury, especially in personal injury cases, because even a small spinal cord or brain injury can have long lasting and far-reaching effects.

Despite the advancements in technology and treatment options, neurosurgery remains a challenging field. Dr. Singh acknowledges that the complexity of the human brain and spinal cord presents significant obstacles. "The nervous system is incredibly intricate," he explains. "Even with the most advanced tools and techniques, there is always a level of uncertainty in neurosurgery. Our goal is to minimize risks and achieve the best possible outcomes for our patients."

Dr. Singh also points to the emotional and psychological challenges faced by patients undergoing neurosurgical procedures. "Patients often experience anxiety and fear when they are told they need brain or spinal surgery," he says. "It is our job as surgeons to provide not only the technical expertise but also the emotional support and reassurance that they need during this difficult time."

Neurologists can also be valuable in a legal context after someone has experienced a personal injury. Dr. Lawler explains that he works closely with personal injury lawyers to provide accurate medical information and expert opinions. "We are happy to discuss the case with the attorney, provide medical records, update on any treatment recommendations, and if warranted, provide an expert report detailing our treatment," he explained. This collaboration ensures that both plaintiff and defense attorneys receive objective and expert assessments of their clients' conditions.

Dr. Shah describes how navigating through medical systems, particularly regarding injuries, is undeniably challenging and defines several obstacles he has seen during his career. First and foremost is the complexity of filing a claim. Many patients, especially those involved in car collisions, are unaware of how to file a claim with their car insurance or set up a meeting with a case manager to help navigate the system.

The second challenge involves medical professionals. Due to the complexity of the system and the significant administrative support required, many doctors are reluctant to invest in the necessary resources. This reluctance often leads to limited access to care for these patients.

The third major obstacle is insurance coverage. In New Jersey, for example, it operates under a no-fault state system, meaning that expenses initially go through car insurance. Often, just the ambulance ride and an emergency room visit can deplete the available funds from the insurance plan. Dr. Shah asks, "What happens next for patients without health insurance, or those whose insurance isn't accepted, such as Medicaid?" This situation significantly hinders their ability to receive care.

These issues prevent patients from seeking care. Patients with attorneys who prioritize patient care, however, tend to receive better treatment. The fact that a referral comes from an attorney does not diminish its validity. Neurologists receive referrals from laypeople all the time, and they are treated with the same regard. "Our goal is to help people navigate through the system to ensure they receive the best possible care and can get back on their feet. If we determine we cannot assist a patient, we are transparent with them and their attorney about the limitations of what we can provide."

Dr. Shah emphasizes, "It is crucial to choose the right representative and to work with doctors who not only treat patients properly but also understand how to navigate the system through their administrative capabilities."

Neurologists play a vital role in the management and treatment of personal injury victims with brain and spinal cord injuries. Their expertise extends beyond clinical care to include navigating the complexities of the healthcare system, providing personalized and multidisciplinary treatment plans, and offering crucial support to patients and their families. Advancements in technology, such as minimally invasive surgery and neuro-monitoring, alongside emphasizing the importance of early intervention and patient tailored treatment approaches, have all significantly improved patient outcomes.

Neurologists' collaboration with personal injury lawyers further highlights their critical role in ensuring accurate medical evaluations and supporting the legal process. Understanding the intricacies and varied nature of these injuries is essential, as even seemingly minor injuries can have profound and lasting effects. As such, the comprehensive care provided by neurologists is indispensable in helping patients recover and regain their quality of life.

Visiting a neurologist or neurosurgeon after experiencing a personal injury is crucial for anyone who suspects a brain injury. Early and accurate diagnosis can significantly alter the outcome, helping to mitigate long-term damage and facilitate a more effective recovery. Dr. Shah's insights not only shed light on the complexities of brain injuries but also emphasize the essential role of specialized care in the aftermath of such events.

TAKEAWAYS FROM THIS CHAPTER

1. **Urgency of Treatment:** The chapter emphasizes the critical nature of timely medical intervention following a brain or spinal injury. Immediate assessment and treatment by specialists like neurologists or neurosurgeons are essential for mitigating long-term damage and enhancing recovery outcomes. Dr. Shah and Dr. Lawler both underscore the necessity of addressing brain injuries "as quickly as possible" to ensure the most effective care.

2. **Multidisciplinary Approach:** A multidisciplinary approach is vital in the treatment of brain and spinal injuries. This approach involves various specialists, including neurologists, neurosurgeons, physiatrists, and sports medicine doctors, who collaborate to provide a comprehensive treatment plan tailored to the individual needs of the patient.

3. **Spectrum of Brain Injuries:** There is a wide spectrum of brain injuries, from catastrophic cases requiring emergency surgery to non-surgical cases like concussions. This diversity in injury types highlights the versatile role of neurosurgeons in managing both surgical and non-surgical brain health issues.

4. **Personalized Treatment Plans:** Treatment for brain and spinal injuries must be personalized. The chapter points out that no single treatment algorithm fits all patients; instead, care plans must be customized based on the unique circumstances and specific needs of each patient, as articulated by Dr. Lawler and Dr. Shah.

5. **Importance of Early and Accurate Diagnosis:** Early and accurate diagnosis in the management of brain injuries is vital. Comprehensive evaluations, including physical examinations and imaging studies like MRI and CAT scans, are crucial for developing effective treatment strategies. This diagnostic process also involves a clinical correlation performed by the neurosurgeon to integrate imaging findings with clinical symptoms for a precise treatment plan.

Gregory J. Lawler, D.O., is a Board Certified Anesthesiologist and Interventional Pain Management Physician specializing in treating neck and low back pain using minimally invasive techniques. He is skilled in advanced pain management procedures, including discography, epidurals, radiofrequency, and spinal cord stimulation. Dr. Lawler holds hospital privileges for assisting in cervical and lumbar discectomy/fusion surgeries.

Recognized as a leading expert in pain management, Dr. Lawler has been featured on CBS-2 New York and honored with titles such as "America's Best Physician" and "Leading Physician of the World." He teaches at Touro College of Osteopathic Medical School and is actively involved in professional organizations like the American Society of Pain Medicine and the North American Spine Society.

— WWW.NORTHJERSEYINTERVENTIONALPAIN.COM —

Harshpal Singh, M.D., is a board-certified neurosurgeon with advanced subspecialized training in neuro-radiology and complex and minimally invasive spinal surgery. He has extensive experience treating a broad range of complex patient conditions using the latest treatment approaches.

Dr. Singh attended medical school at the Medical College of Georgia and completed a residency at Mount Sinai School of Medicine, where he served as Chief Resident. During his fellowship training at the University of Miami, Dr. Singh focused on treating spinal cord injuries, severe spinal trauma, and complex cervical spine deformities. He is also highly experienced in treating neurological head trauma and general neurosurgery. His clinical research has centered on spinal fusion and complex revision spinal surgery.

— WWW.PREMIERSPINENJ.COM —

Nirav K. Shah, M.D., FAANS, FACS, is a dedicated neurosurgeon passionate about treating patients with brain and spine disorders. His journey in medicine began early when he was accepted into the accelerated premedical-medical program at Penn State University, where he discovered his calling in neurosurgery. Drawn to the discipline by the intense challenges and dedication of the neurosurgeons he admired, Dr. Shah has embraced the high stakes and pressures of the field, finding fulfillment in his work.

As the medical director of Princeton Brain, Spine & Sports Medicine, Dr. Shah approaches each patient with empathy, treating them as individuals rather than just medical cases.

— WWW.PRINCETONBRAINANDSPINE.COM —

Edward H. Scheid, M.D., FAANS, is an accomplished spine surgeon with over 5,000 successful surgeries to his name. He prioritizes a conservative approach and thoroughly examines each patient to identify the root cause of their pain before considering surgery. His individualized treatment plans are designed to alleviate discomfort and enhance quality of life.

Specializing in reoperative spine surgery and spinal cord stimulation, Dr. Scheid has extensive experience helping patients who have yet to find success with traditional spine surgeries. His expertise has earned him recognition from prestigious organizations such as the American Association of Neurological Surgeons and North American Spine Society.

— WWW.NORTHEASTSPINEANDSPORTS.COM —

Chapter 7

HOW ECONOMISTS PROVE FINANCIAL LOSSES

"What I wish more people understood is the impact that injuries have on a person's ability to do more than just work."

— KRISTIN KUCSMA

PERSONAL INJURY LAW presents a unique blend of challenges and responsibilities that go beyond the courtroom. In the intricate realm of personal injury litigation, quantifying economic damages demands not only a sophisticated blend of analytical skills and deep economic knowledge but also an understanding of the legal landscape, including client-lawyer relationships and the negotiation dynamics with insurance companies. This is a complex process involving individuals who are often facing the most difficult period of their lives.

Kristin Kucsma, a distinguished economic expert, argues a comprehensive approach to evaluating economic damages includes assessing lost compensation, the cost of lifetime care, and the impact on the ability to perform various services, demonstrating the meticulous nature of her work.

The process begins with an evaluation of lost compensation. Kucsma details, "I examine the type of work the injured person was doing before the injury, how much money they were earning, and any fringe benefits they may have been receiving, such as health insurance and retirement benefits." This initial assessment, while seemingly straightforward, often requires a deep dive into complex compensation structures, especially in cases involving union workers or C-suite executives with equity-based compensations.

For instance, evaluating the value of a union worker's benefits involves delving into union documents and collective bargaining agreements. Conversely, cases involving C-suite executives or those receiving equity compensation, such as stock options or restricted stock units, necessitate a different approach. Kucsma elaborates, "Evaluating these compensation packages requires a deep dive into various documents and agreements to accurately determine the financial impact of the injury."

In cases involving young individuals or those in the early stages of their careers, Kucsma employs statistical data to project potential earnings. For example, if a recent college graduate is injured, Kucsma analyzes career progression data based on education levels and industry standards to estimate future earnings. Similarly, for individuals likely to have received promotions she considers potential career advancements that might have been realized in their future. She explains, "We also work on many situations in which a plaintiff likely would have been promoted if they had not been injured. For example, we work on many cases involving law enforcement officers. Suppose the plaintiff was a patrol officer at the time of their injury, but it was anticipated that they would have been promoted to sergeant and perhaps even to the rank of lieutenant. This is something else that we need to flesh out."

The second category Kucsma addresses is the cost of lifetime care. This involves assessing the future medical needs of the injured person, which can include therapies, medications, surgeries, and other medical interventions. Kucsma emphasizes, "My role is to analyze this information from the Life Care Planner and account for the effects of inflation and the increasing cost of medical care over the plaintiff's remaining life expectancy."

To achieve this, Kucsma relies on Life Care Plans or medical narratives provided by specialists. Her task is to incorporate inflation factors and project future costs accurately for each individual. For instance, in New Jersey, she may reduce future costs to their present value, a practice not universally applied in other jurisdictions. This meticulous approach ensures that the financial projections align with real-world economic conditions. Kucsma explains, "When evaluating the cost of lifetime care, my role is relatively limited. I use the expert opinions of others as my starting point. I am provided with a report that identifies the types of care a person will need, including medications, surgeries, therapies, and so on. I rely on another expert for information about the frequency of care and for their opinion on the current costs of care."

One of the more nuanced aspects of proving damages involves valuing services that the injured person can no longer perform. This can range from household chores and maintenance to childcare services. Kucsma explains, "It is interesting to note that economists have been valuing these types of services for well over 100 years, predating litigation. We can objectively value these services by identifying strangers in the marketplace who provide similar services."

For example, if an injured person could no longer perform yard work or childcare, the cost of hiring professionals to perform these tasks must be calculated. This method allows her to assign a monetary value to services that family members typically provide without charge. By examining the cost of hiring outside help, she can provide a clear economic assessment of the lost services. Kucsma elucidates, "Pain and suffering have no impact on my analysis, and I think it's very important for attorneys and juries to recognize that. For example, I do not assign a value to pain and suffering, nor do I inflate the value of any economic damages. I simply evaluate what one would pay a stranger in the marketplace to perform these services, which allows me to objectively assess them."

In cases where the ability to return to work is in question, collaboration with vocational experts is vital. These experts evaluate the injured person's capacity to work and provide opinions on potential job opportunities and earnings. Kucsma notes, "Involving a vocational expert may be worthwhile to gain a more comprehensive understanding of the situation. Vocational experts can offer insights into whether the injured person can return to their previous job or find alternative employment."

Vocational experts can assess various scenarios, such as a reduction in earning capacity or the ability to perform different types of work post-injury. This collaboration helps create a more accurate and detailed economic damage assessment.

The economic expert should be able to handle complex data and prepare for testimony in court. In preparing for trials, Kucsma often reviews reports from other experts and anticipates key areas of questioning. For example, she prepares for cross-examination by ensuring she has all the necessary documents and understands the economic principles underlying her analyses. This preparation is crucial, especially when dealing with complex cases involving high-income earners or intricate compensation structures. Kucsma explains, "When preparing my reports and getting ready for trial, I think about the types of questions I would pose if I were working with the defense attorney."

Effective evaluation of economic damages depends heavily on detailed and accurate documentation. Kucsma advises attorneys to provide comprehensive information, including W-2 wage and tax statements, union documents, and tax returns. She notes, "For W-2 workers, such as police officers or union plumbers, the W-2 wage and tax statements are typically more informative than tax returns. This is because tax returns often do not reflect tax-deferred compensation."

In cases involving self-employed individuals or independent contractors, tax returns become essential for assessing compensation. Kucsma emphasizes the importance of understanding the unique facts of each case and gathering all relevant documents to ensure a thorough evaluation.

Being an economic expert in personal injury cases involves a complex interplay of analyzing lost compensation, projecting lifetime care costs, and valuing services. A meticulous approach and collaboration with vocational experts ensure a comprehensive assessment of economic damages. By leveraging her extensive experience and background in economics, Kucsma navigates the intricacies of each case, providing valuable insights that contribute to fair and accurate compensation for injured individuals.

In every case, from catastrophic injuries to young individuals at the start of their careers, the work of an economic expert underscores the importance of detailed analysis and thorough documentation. The role of economic experts is critical in the legal process, with their work helping to ensure that justice is served. Kucsma argues, "It's also important to remember that experienced economic experts bring more than just economic knowledge. I've testified over 400 times in federal and state trials and have been deposed over 700 times."

Ultimately, the economic assessments and strategies discussed in this chapter serve as a critical component in the pursuit of justice within the realm of personal injury law. They underscore the importance of expert analysis in bridging the gap between legal theory and practical, life-changing impacts on individuals. As such, economic experts play an indispensable role in shaping outcomes that are not only legally sound but also deeply attuned to the personal circumstances and the future well-being of those they serve.

TAKEAWAYS FROM THIS CHAPTER

1. **Comprehensive Damage Assessment:** Economic experts play a crucial role in personal injury cases by providing a comprehensive evaluation of economic damages. This includes assessing lost compensation, future medical needs, and the monetary value of services the injured person can no longer perform.

2. **Deep Analysis of Compensation Structures:** Evaluating economic damages requires a detailed examination of the injured person's compensation, including wages, benefits, and potential career progression. This is particularly complex for individuals with intricate compensation packages, such as union workers or C-suite executives.

3. **Lifetime Care Costs:** Economic experts calculate the lifetime care costs of the injured party, considering future medical interventions and adjusting for inflation. This ensures that financial projections remain relevant throughout the injured person's lifespan.

4. **Valuation of Non-Monetary Contributions:** It is vital to give value to services that injured individuals can no longer provide, such as household chores or childcare. Economic experts use market rates to assign a monetary value to these services, ensuring a fair evaluation of all forms of economic loss.

5. **Collaboration with Vocational Experts:** To accurately assess the injured person's capacity to work and future earning potential, economic experts collaborate with vocational experts. This multidisciplinary approach provides a more complete picture of the economic impact of the injury, enabling a more precise calculation of damages.

Kristin Kucsma is the Managing Director and Chief Economist at Sobel Tinari Economics Group, where she leads a team of economists and analysts. Since joining in 2008, Kris has worked on various cases, including personal injury, wrongful death, and employment law. Her expertise has made her a respected expert witness, with over 1,200 depositions and trial testimonies in state and federal courts.

Kristin analyzes economic losses, including lost earnings, lifetime care costs, and complex fringe benefits. She is also a frequent lecturer on valuing economic damages. Before joining Sobel Tinari, Kris taught economics at several universities, including Rutgers and Seton Hall. For ten consecutive years, the New York Law Journal readers have recognized her as the #1 individual expert witness in economics.

— WWW.SOBELTINARIECONOMICS.COM —

Chapter 8

HOW TO AVOID BEING A VICTIM IN YOUR PERSONAL INJURY CASE

PERSONAL INJURY CASES are inherently challenging, not just because of the physical and emotional toll they take, but also because of the potential pitfalls that can turn you, the injured party, into a victim a second time. The legal process can be overwhelming, and without the right knowledge and preparation, it's easy to make mistakes that could jeopardize your case. This chapter will guide you through the steps to ensure you remain in control, avoid common traps, and protect your rights throughout your personal injury case.

To successfully navigate the complexities of a personal injury case, it's essential to recognize that the power to protect your rights and secure fair compensation lies in your hands. While the legal process may seem disconcerting, taking charge early on can make a world of difference. By understanding the importance of your initial actions and being vigilant in your approach, you can set the foundation for a strong case and prevent further victimization.

The first step in avoiding victimization in a personal injury case is to take control of your situation from the outset. This means being proactive in seeking medical attention, documenting everything, and understanding that you are not powerless. The actions you take immediately following can significantly influence the outcome of your case.

For example, if you're involved in a car crash, make sure to gather as much evidence as possible at the scene. Take photographs of the vehicles involved, the surrounding area, and any visible injuries you've sustained. Collect contact information from witnesses and make a note of any details that might be relevant later. By taking control early on, you're setting the foundation for a strong case and ensuring that you have the necessary evidence to support your claims.

In addition to gathering evidence, it's crucial to understand the value of standing firm in the face of pressure. The evidence you collect is your shield against those who may try to undermine your claim. As you move forward, remember that you have the right to pursue fair compensation and should not feel compelled to accept less than what you deserve. Maintaining confidence in your case and being prepared to assert your rights will help you navigate the challenges ahead.

It's important to recognize that you have rights and that you deserve fair treatment. Insurance companies and opposing parties may attempt to minimize your claim or pressure you into accepting a quick, lowball settlement. Don't be afraid to stand up for yourself and demand what you deserve.

Remember, the first offer you receive from an insurance company is often far below what your case is actually worth. They're hoping that you'll accept it out of desperation or a desire to put the incident behind you. Instead of accepting the first offer, consult with a qualified personal injury lawyer who can help you determine the true value of your case and negotiate on your behalf.

Understanding that the first offer is likely inadequate is just the beginning. It's also essential to remain cautious when dealing with insurance adjusters, as their tactics are designed to benefit the company, not you. By consulting with a personal injury lawyer early on, you can avoid falling into common traps and ensure that your interactions with the insurance company don't compromise your case. This professional guidance is crucial in navigating the complex strategies insurance adjusters may use to minimize your claim.

Insurance adjusters' primary goal is to protect the insurance company's bottom line, not to ensure that you receive fair compensation. They may employ various tactics to gather information that could be used against you later, such as asking seemingly innocent questions or offering a quick settlement.

Be cautious when speaking with insurance adjusters. Provide only the necessary information, and whenever possible, direct them to your attorney. By doing so, you're protecting yourself from inadvertently saying something that could harm your case later on.

Taking precautions when dealing with insurance adjusters is essential, but safeguarding your case doesn't stop there. To truly protect your rights and maximize your chances of a favorable outcome, securing the right legal representation is paramount. A skilled personal injury lawyer will not only handle communications with the insurance company but also provide the expertise and advocacy needed to navigate the complexities of your case, ensuring that your interests are always prioritized and that you're treated fairly.

When choosing a lawyer, it's important to select someone who specializes in personal injury law and has experience handling cases similar to yours. A certified civil trial lawyer, for example, has undergone rigorous training and testing to demonstrate their expertise in trial law. They are equipped to handle the complexities of your case and can help you navigate the legal system with confidence.

While finding the right lawyer is a critical step in protecting your interests, it's also important to be mindful of how your actions outside the courtroom can affect your case. In particular, social media has become a powerful tool that can either support or undermine your claims.

In today's digital age, social media can be a double-edged sword. While it's a great way to stay connected with friends and family, it can also be a minefield for personal injury victims. Insurance companies and opposing parties often scour social media profiles looking for evidence that can be used to discredit your claims.

For example, if you post photos of yourself engaging in activities that seem inconsistent with your claimed injuries, it could harm your case. Even innocent posts can be taken out of context and used against you. To avoid this, it's best to limit your social media activity during the course of your case and avoid posting anything related to the incident, your injuries, or your recovery. Always assume that anything you post could be seen by the opposing party.

While being cautious with your social media activity is essential to protecting your case, it's equally important to prioritize your physical recovery. Adhering to your doctor's recommendations and attending all medical appointments is not only vital for your health but also plays a significant role in demonstrating the seriousness of your injuries. Any lapses in your medical care could be used by the opposing party to downplay the extent of your injuries, potentially jeopardizing your claim. Failing to follow medical advice or missing appointments can be used against you to suggest that your injuries aren't as severe as you claim.

Document all of your medical treatments, attend all scheduled appointments, and follow through with any recommended therapies or procedures. This will not only aid in your recovery but also strengthen your case by showing that you're taking your injuries seriously and doing everything possible to recover.

The legal process can be slow, and it's easy to become frustrated or impatient. However, rushing to settle your case too quickly can result in receiving far less compensation than you deserve. Insurance companies often rely on this impatience to pressure victims into accepting lowball offers.

As you diligently document your medical treatments and follow your doctor's advice, it's important to remember that the legal process requires patience. While your focus on recovery is essential, so is allowing the necessary time for your case to develop fully. Rushing through the process can lead to settling for less than what your case is truly worth. By staying patient and resisting the urge to accept quick settlements, you give your attorney the opportunity to negotiate a fair and just compensation that reflects the true extent of your injuries and losses.

Trust in the process and allow your attorney to negotiate the best possible outcome for you. Remember, settlements reached too quickly are often not in the best interest of the victim, and waiting for the right settlement can make a significant difference in your financial recovery.

Knowledge is power, and understanding the personal injury process can help you avoid common pitfalls and make informed decisions. Take the time to educate yourself about your rights, the legal process, and what to expect as your case progresses.

Ask your attorney to explain any aspects of the case that you don't understand and don't be afraid to ask questions. The more informed you are, the less likely you are to be taken advantage of by insurance companies or opposing parties.

By staying informed and actively participating in your case, you can better protect your interests, and one of the most effective ways to do so is by keeping detailed records of all relevant information. This includes medical bills, receipts for expenses related to the injury, correspondence with insurance companies, and any other documents that could be relevant.

These records will be invaluable to your attorney when building your case and can help ensure that you receive compensation for all your expenses, including those that may not be immediately obvious, such as transportation costs to medical appointments or modifications to your home to accommodate your injuries.

Finally, it's important to know when to say no. Whether it's an insurance company pressuring you to settle for less than you deserve, or someone advising you to take actions that don't feel right to you, trust your instincts and don't be afraid to stand your ground. Your lawyer will provide guidance, but ultimately, the decisions in your case are yours to make. Don't let anyone pressure you into making decisions that aren't in your best interest. Saying no when it matters most can help you avoid becoming a victim in your personal injury case.

Being involved in a personal injury case can be an overwhelming experience, but it doesn't mean you have to be a victim. By taking control of your situation, standing up for yourself, and making informed decisions, you can navigate the process with confidence and protect your rights. With the right legal representation, patience, and persistence, you can achieve the best possible outcome and ensure that you receive the compensation you deserve.

TAKEAWAYS FROM THIS CHAPTER

1. Take Control Early On: The actions you take immediately following a personal injury, such as seeking medical attention and gathering evidence, are crucial in setting the foundation for a strong personal injury case and avoiding victimization.

2. Don't Trust Insurance Adjusters: Insurance adjusters aim to minimize payouts. By providing only necessary information and directing them to your attorney, you protect your case from being undermined.

3. Hire the Right Legal Representation: Choosing a lawyer who specializes in personal injury law and has relevant experience ensures that you have the expertise needed to navigate the legal process and secure fair compensation.

4. Mind Your Social Media Activity: Social media can be used against you in a personal injury case. Limiting your activity and avoiding posts related to your injuries or recovery is essential to protect your claim.

5. Prioritize Medical Treatment and Documentation: Following your doctor's advice, attending all appointments, and documenting your medical treatments not only aids in your recovery but also strengthens your case by demonstrating the seriousness of your injuries.

WHAT'S NEXT?

THANK YOU FOR READING THIS BOOK. I trust you found the information to be as informative and thought-provoking as I did.

I hope this book showed you the importance of having the right team in place after being involved in a personal injury. My goal was to empower you to seek out the right medical professionals and find the right lawyer to help you get the outcome you deserve. I want anyone who has been injured to know they aren't alone, and that there is a way through one of the most difficult things anyone can go through.

My intent was to give you the information necessary to make smart choices after experiencing a personal injury. I want to help you get on the right path to lead to a successful outcome in your case.

If you have any follow up questions after any chapter, please feel free to reach out to the experts I interviewed. Their contact information will be at the end of the chapter they are featured in.

Because you purchased this book, you can reach out to me for a

complimentary personal injury legal consult. I will be happy to answer any questions you might have. If you decide to take advantage of this offer, my contact information is on the next page.

CONTACT US

COMPLIMENTARY

VICTIM TO VICTORY

Personal Injury Consulation

CONTACT

Lawrence A. LeBrocq, Esq.

CEO & MANAGING PARTNER

PHONE
855 GGL WINS

WEB
www.gglwins.com

EMAIL
info@gglwins.com

OVER $1 BILLION Recovered For Our Clients

GGL
CARLES GRABLER & LEBROCQ PC
INJURY LAWYERS

Made in the USA
Monee, IL
21 June 2025